DALE SPENDER

THERE'S ALWAY'S BEEN A WOMEN'S MOVEMENT THIS CENTURY

Dale Spender is an Australian feminist, living and working in London. Her many books include *Women of Ideas* (1982); *Man Made Language* (1981); *Invisible Women* (1982); *Men's Studies Modified* (editor, 1981); *Learning to Lose: Sexism and Education* (co-editor, with Elizabeth Sarah, 1980). She is also editor of the journal *Women's Studies International Forum.*

Cover Illustrator Christine MacCauley is a painter, illustrator and teacher who lives in London. She has done graphics work for *Spare Rib* since it was founded and has illustrated book jackets for The Women's Press.

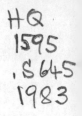
Dale Spender to Mary Stott

'And tell me Mary, what did you do during the time
when there was no women's movement?'

Mary Stott, with great indignation,

'What do you mean, when there was *no* women's movement?
THERE'S ALWAYS BEEN A WOMEN'S MOVEMENT
THIS CENTURY!'

DALE SPENDER

THERE'S ALWAYS BEEN A WOMEN'S MOVEMENT THIS CENTURY

PANDORA PRESS

Routledge & Kegan Paul
London, Boston, Melbourne and Henley

First published in 1983
by Pandora Press,
(Routledge & Kegan Paul Plc)
39 Store Street, London WC1E 7DD,
9 Park Street, Boston, Mass. 02108, USA,
296 Beaconsfield Parade, Middle Park,
Melbourne, 3206, Australia, and
Broadway House, Newtown Road,
Henley-on-Thames, Oxon RG9 1EN
Photoset in 10 on 11½ Century Schoolbook by
Kelly Typesetting Ltd, Bradford-on-Avon, Wilts
and printed in Great Britain by
St Edmundsbury Press, Bury St Edmunds, Suffolk

Library of Congress Cataloging in Publication Data

Spender, Dale.

There's always been a women's movement this century.

Bibliography: p.
1. Feminists – Great Britain – Biography.
2. Feminists – United States – Biography.
3. Feminism – Great Britain – History – 20th century.
4. Feminism – United States – History – 20th century. I. Title.
HQ1595.S645 1983   305.4'2'0973   82–22574

ISBN 0–86358–002–5

B + N   5,95 | 2/6/84

CONTENTS

ILLUSTRATIONS

Plates between pages 88–89

ACKNOWLEDGMENTS

It goes without saying that this book could never have been undertaken without the generous co-operation of Hazel Hunkins Hallinan, Rebecca West, Dora Russell, Mary Stott, and Constance Rover. I am grateful not only for the time they gave me (along with the hospitality and refreshments) but for the rich dimension they have added to my life.

And I am grateful to the Fawcett Library and its helpful librarians, Catherine Ireland and David Doughan, who have not only willingly helped me find much background material but who in their commitment to women's words make their own invaluable contribution to preserving and structuring women's past.

To Harriet Griffey I owe much – not just for the tedious work involved in obtaining 'permissions', but for her support and good cheer.

I have also been fortunate in the 'feedback' that I have received as this book has been written and I want to express great thanks to Glynis Wood who not only typed the manuscript but who provided a running commentary on her response. Her enthusiasm – and her eagerness for the next 'super old lady' – have certainly added much pleasure to the solitary task of writing.

I also want to thank my mother – who while she may not appreciate it – is another 'super old lady' who has taught me (indirectly at times) the fallacy of the belief that it is the young who have all the answers.

Acknowledgment and thanks are due for the assistance given by The Mansell Collection, *The Daily Telegraph*, *The Guardian*, *Punch*, Radio Times Hulton Picture Library, Stephen Peet and Christopher Cook in the location of, and permission to reproduce, the illustrations.

For Hazel Hunkins Hallinan 1890–1982

'In her honour we should dedicate ourselves anew to finishing our own liberation.'

INTRODUCTION
Lighting the corridors of history

'Women have no history', said Virginia Woolf in 1929. History 'is the history of the male line'. Men have encoded the events of their lives, written them down, passed them on and constructed a visible, active and glorious line of male descent. But for women the past is a silence, an absence: the pattern of women's lives 'lies at present locked in old diaries, stuffed away in old drawers, half obliterated in the memories of the aged'. The corridors of history are for women, unlit, said Virginia Woolf, and 'the figures of generations of women are so dimly, so fitfully perceived' (p. 141).

I grew up in a world where women were without a history. I felt a distinct sense of loss. I also felt considerable discomfort and distress. The idea that women have no past *because they have contributed nothing of value to our culture* is an easy one to implant in the minds of both sexes in our society, but the idea has different repercussions for boys than it does for girls. For both sexes it helps to 'explain' the world, it helps to justify male dominance: while this may be a self-enhancing understanding for boys it can become a self-denying one for girls. For me, the recognition that women had no positive past produced doubts and apprehensions about the present and the future.

Sad and regrettable, I thought, tragic that women have had so few opportunities to exercise their human potential; unfair, I thought, that women should have been so weighed down by considerations of 'womanliness' that they should have been prevented from participating in public life: dreadful, I thought, that women should have been so burdened with domestic duties, so wearied by repeated pregnancies that the major task was to get through the day, to survive. Working-class women who have contended with the double shift of the home and the workplace; black women who have had to 'serve their masters' twenty-four hours a day, who have been brutally treated – how sad, how wasteful that there was nothing 'left over', I thought. No time, no energy, no desire for poetry, philosophy, politics, music, art ...

drudgery, dreariness, and the battle to survive are not the stuff from which cultural inspiration and energy springs.

Sad and regrettable – but *the past*! There was no necessity for this pattern to be repeated, I argued with myself. Were we not a new generation of women with raised consciousness? We could and we would change the patterns of the past: we could and we would be the *first* to claim our full female humanity! The divisions of private/public, home/work would be broken down, there would be a more equitable division of labour – and resources – and we would ensure our contribution to the new way of life in which the creative and imaginative resources of the *whole* population were utilised. We would begin the battle for women's liberation and future generations of women would not contemplate a womanless past.

How easily, completely – and unsuspectingly – I fell into the trap!

Feminism has for me been a journey, and I did not find out overnight that I was travelling down the wrong road. I must admit that even in my youthful feminist days I had begun to be suspicious of the directions society gave me, of the signposts it provided. I started to make detours, to pursue paths clearly marked 'Danger' and 'Trespassers Will Be Prosecuted' – even signs which warned that only the foolish would want to enter. But it was women's *silence*, women's absence that interested me, and I continued in my travels even though there were many experts who tried to block my way and who repeatedly assured me that what I was looking for did not exist. Perversity, however, can be productive in a patriarchal society.

I followed the trail of women's silence. I followed it in women's conversation with men: I followed women's silence in education and I followed women's silence in the encoded knowledge of our society. And it was not long before women's silence was of deafening and resounding significance for me.

Reared on womanless education it was sheer joy to discover that the lights in the corridors of history could be turned on and that the 'dimly and fitfully perceived' women could be startlingly illuminated. The excitement was intense – but the anger began to burn.

Defying the signs that said 'conservative and unattractive women, interested only in the vote' and 'dead end, particularly dull scenery', I followed the path of earlier women's movements and found among the many energising and empowering women, one in particular who captured my imagination – Elizabeth Cady Stanton.

She was superb. I read everything I could about her. I read what she wrote. I deplored the fact that I had so many questions I wanted to ask her and no way of finding her answers – for there is no great body of literature about her! She is not on the highway of human affairs of the past! I laughed with her, and anguished with her, and puzzled with her.

And I began to feel disorientated. Here she was – more than a century ago – making a momentous contribution to our culture, but she had been by-passed. I began to have niggling doubts that *we* could hardly be the first generation of women to claim full humanity in the face of the evidence of Elizabeth Cady Stanton's existence.

A mistake, an accident that she had been 'overlooked' I asked myself? Another woman, over a century ago, who had been claiming the same things that we were claiming for women in the name of women's liberation? Another woman who not only shared our claim, but shared our experience that she was among the *first* to make it – and found out that *she* had been misled!

Like us, Elizabeth Cady Stanton felt the loss of a womanless education. She lamented women's absence from the cultural world, and she argued, in the second half of the nineteenth century, that this would change when women were liberated and able to take their full and proper place in society, where they could exercise all their faculties. And her friend, colleague, and co-worker, Matilda Joslyn Gage told her she was talking a lot of nonsense!

It was just totally untrue that women had never contributed to society, said Matilda Joslyn Gage: women had made an enormous contribution – but men had erased it! One of the most radical and courageous philosophers, writers and scholars of the time, Matilda Joslyn Gage had no difficulty in proving that women had achieved in every field of human endeavour: she made massive lists of women's contributions in science, mathematics, medicine, literature, law, politics, philosophy – and even documented women's achievements as inventors, military strategists, and theologians![1]

Sheer wishful thinking on the part of men, nothing but a deliberate device to construct their dominance, that's what this womanless history was, declared Gage. And then she went on to argue – in 1893 – that now that women had laid to rest the myth that they were without a past, there would be no need to face that particular demoralising problem again.

Gone were the days she said, when women would believe they were starting from nothing, that they were the first generation to see the possibility and the challenge of playing a part in the shaping of society.

Yet Matilda Joslyn Gage herself became one of the dimly and fitfully perceived figures in the unlit corridor of women's history, and she was neither the first nor the last feminist to become a victim of the process of erasure – a process she had understood so well and described.

Fifty years after Matilda Joslyn Gage there was another inspirational feminist historian making her presence felt – Mary Ritter Beard. Women have always been a very real force in history she insisted to women who had once more come to believe they were without a past and had no choice but to begin from the beginning. Women, argued Mary Ritter Beard, have been active and competent through the ages – and it is devastating for us if we do not understand this! If we believe we are without a past, she said, our collective strength is undermined, and the idea that we are inferior takes hold of our minds and helps to construct the bonds of our oppression. If women are to be liberated, she argued passionately, then they must *know* that they *do* have a forceful, valuable and marvellous past. They must know that they are part of a long constructive tradition, that there is a collective, historical experience of women which is a strength to be drawn upon, she asserted. And then this utter absurdity – that women must start from nothing and take the first tentative and doubtful steps towards full humanity – will be exposed for the absurdity that it is, and will lose the power that it has over our minds.

Twenty years later I was doing my womanless history course at university without the slightest suspicion that there had been women like Mary Ritter Beard, Ray Strachey, Matilda Joslyn Gage, Margaret Fuller, Harriet Martineau, Frances Wright, Catherine Macaulay, Mary Astell or Aphra Behn.[2] I did not know that women had a rich and resourcing history and that the information I was receiving in my history course had been rigorously censored. I did not know that virtually all the reference to positive women had been removed, and that what I was being provided with was among the most partisan, distorted and highly edited material that any ruling group had ever distributed in the interest of retaining its ruling power. I thought I was being taught the truth and I was being fed political propaganda.

It worked! It did undermine, it did introduce doubts; it did suggest if women were to accomplish anything then it would have to be in the future.

And so along with most if not all of my generation I came to share an experience historically common to women, of believing that we were the first generation to make the radical claim for full humanity. And again, as so many of our foremothers had done, we looked to the future – but we also began to pick up some of the pieces of the past and to recognise that in a patriarchal society one cannot believe what one is taught.

Virginia Woolf was for me one of the women who illuminated the path: *Three Guineas* is a passionate plea for women to be unbelievers in a male dominated society, and *A Room of One's Own* is – among other things – a conscious attempt to construct women's traditions. It is an attempt to show that far from being the first we have a legacy of a long, meaningful and continuous past. Virginia Woolf wanted to explore her roots as a woman writer, to find out where she belonged and where she could go and she cast her light on women writers of earlier times, she brought them out of the shadows where they were but dimly and fitfully perceived. With her imaginative art of returning to 'lost' women she helped to show us how we can forge the links between one generation and the next, construct our continuity and *make* our own tradition in a patriarchal world which has made women's heritage invisible.

I learnt much from Virginia Woolf and I was for a while content to think that the task was to return to women, long 'lost', and to breathe some life into them, to invest them with substance. 'Imagination' played a crucial role in her recreation of women's tradition, and in the pattern that she had set it was no great leap to speculate on what it would be like, for example, to meet Aphra Behn or talk to Anne Finch, two women writers who became models for Virginia Woolf. And with Woolf as my model I did my own share of 'imagining'. I thought of the questions I would like to ask her, the discussions I would have with Mary Ritter Beard, the gossiping I would engage in with Matilda Joslyn Gage. I even thought it would be a splendid idea to write a play – a party where so many of our foremothers gathered together and compared notes: there was enough evidence available to reconstruct much of the dialogue. . . .

And it was while I was thinking about the guest list, using some of the sources from earlier this century, that I realised that there was no need to 'imagine' my conversations with Dora Russell and Rebecca West.

The astonishment with which I suddenly recognised that Dora Russell and Rebecca West were not women of the past but women of the present is hard to convey now. It even seemed so silly that I had not thought to seek out these women, to meet with them, talk with them, question them. There was the sheer absurdity of the fact that we of the post-sixties women's movement had *ignored* this rich resource of their experience, and our omission required some explanation.

I understood that by *not* seeking them out we had contributed to their invisibility, that we had played a role in the denial of women's existence and strength. I understood that a male dominated society will not forge for us the links between one generation of women and the next and that unless we take matters into our own hands and actively make those links we are just as effectively divided from older women, as we are from women of the past.

It was – and is – clear to me that in a patriarchal society

women have little control over the knowledge we produce. We have been producing our knowledge for centuries but it has been kept out of the socially valued reservoir of knowledge which is transmitted from one generation to the next, and made the substance of the educational curriculum. Our own history, where we have been able to find it and put it together, tells us again and again that women have generated explanations about the world – and about male power and how it is constructed and how it can be undermined – and again and again those explanations have been *edited out*, erased, so that women are initiated into a society which convinces them that nothing has gone before and that they must start from scratch.

This pattern is not going to change unless we change it, but to bring about change means that we have to defy much of what we have been taught and which we may see as sensible.

We can begin by acknowledging that sexism isn't something other, horrid people do, but in a sexist society, something that all members do. Sexism is a code that we learn and operate and while feminists are trying to make that code explicit, to resist it and cease using it, we are not immune. Life as a feminist can be a daily process of discovery of yet more sexist rules that one is operating, and for me, the rejection of older women comes into this category, for I was bound to admit that by ignoring the elder stateswomen of the women's movement I was operating sexist rules which helped to make them invisible. I was colluding in the erasure of women's tradition.

My education had not, of course, prepared me for the possibility of *wise women*: it had even 'programmed' me to deny them when confronted with the direct evidence of their existence. I also shared the values of a society which suggested that the twentieth century had been a period of unparallelled progress and so I was more than ready to dismiss the insights of previous generations. In my mind there was the conviction that those who had been prominent earlier this century would probably have little of relevance to offer to the present, and along with such prevalent concepts as 'old fashioned' and 'generation gap' the belief was (conveniently) bolstered that those who had fought for women's suffrage were fundamentally conservative, 'reformist' not 'radical', and not concerned with the more contemporary and progressive issues that commanded our attention.

There weren't many patriarchal traps that I did *not* fall into.

Blatant ageism and sexism also caught me out. 'Old women' receive little respect in our society and are more likely to be portrayed as figures of fun than veneration. Even the term 'old woman' is itself often used as a form of abuse. And there are few alternative positive images available to counteract the negative and unattractive image that patriarchy has promulgated.

We have no reality of women as *authorities*, for in a male dominated society the 'experts' are men. Not because men have more 'expertise' as Mary Ritter Beard and countless other women have insisted – but because the expertise of women is denied and ignored. This is why it is so important – they have all argued – that we invest women with authority, that we make women the experts on women's lives and generate a tradition of strong, authoritative women. Such activity is very subversive.

So, with the specific task of making visible what a male dominated society has rendered invisible, I contacted some of our elder stateswomen and they were more than generous in their response. I visited them, talked with them, taped them – and had one of the most satisfying and enjoyable experiences of my life.

I also had a genuine educational experience which stands in stark contrast to much of what I had to endure within formal education, but which helps to suggest what an exciting and invigorating experience learning could be. These 'interviews' are not a research study in the way that knowledge-making has been set up in a patriarchal society – there has been no controlled experiment, no standardisation of questions and for many reasons the five women whose experience provides the data are not a representative sample. But it would be a (patriarchal) mistake to think of these discussions as insignificant but pleasant gossip about old times. This is a form of women's history, a form of women's research in which women are the authorities: it is part of the process of structuring our heritage that society has denied us.

From these women I have learnt so much. I have heard first-hand accounts of the process of reducing women to invisibility and I have been shown how the contributions of youth have been steadily eroded over a lifetime, so that fifty years later they are only dimly and fitfully perceived. I have learnt about the discrimination that has operated against women throughout this century and about – to me – previously unknown women and women's organisations that have consistently campaigned against it. I have heard horror stories of harassment, and passionate pleas for an end to prejudice.

I have also learned much about humour – about the will to continue and the need for optimism. And I have seen comradeship and courage and compassion. By these five women I have been challenged, comforted and cheered: I have had the privilege of listening to wise words and the benefit of being given sound advice.

These five women comprise but a fragment of our past. Although they have all been members of different women's movements, their diversity is by no means the whole and we still have much to learn from those who instead of becoming invisible over time, were never visible in the first place. However, while many other women remain in the shadows we have nonetheless made a start when we have five women who are no longer only dimly and fitfully perceived.

While each woman tells her own story, it is not the whole story: perhaps in other company they would have spoken of different things, perhaps there are issues which they thought important but which I omitted to raise. Yet despite all the many limitations, we have here a valuable record and one which we can use.

During the time that I have been writing this book, Hazel Hunkins Hallinan has died. As some measure of my esteem for her, I wish to dedicate this book to her. It was she who said in commemoration of her friend, Alice Paul, that in her honour we should dedicate ourselves anew to finishing our own liberation. I use her words now, in her honour – 'we should dedicate ourselves anew to finishing our own liberation'. We have such a tradition to live up to.

HAZEL HUNKINS HALLINAN
1890–1982

After a decade of publication, *Spare Rib* has put together an anthology: when issues are sometimes forgotton, when debates shift and when the paper used in such magazines, is not designed for posterity, it is important to bring together some of the evidence of the last ten years which can serve now as a reminder, and in the future as a record. However, while I readily acknowledged the necessity and the value of the *Spare Rib Reader* (edited by Marsha Rowe, 1982), I did not suspect when I opened its pages that it was about to teach me a significant and salutary lesson about women's traditions – and the way they so readily and so easily become invisible in our society.

My attention was drawn immediately to the last article in the book 'Decades: Talking Across the Century: Gail Lewis and Hazel Hunkins Hallinan talking with Carole Spedding and Amanda Sebastyen'. I was surprised. For the last six months I had been following up every reference I could find to Hazel Hunkins Hallinan; *Spare Rib* appeared regularly in the post every month and was eagerly pounced upon by me – and yet I had no recollection of ever having read an article about her. I was even more surprised with what she had had to say to Amanda Sebastyen.

'Germaine Greer's book does me proud on the first and second pages, thanking me for backing the movement when it was so unpopular', she had said in 1980. Germaine Greer? But I also thought I had read everything *she* had ever written, and I couldn't remember anything about Hazel Hunkins Hallinan. I went to my much used copy of *The Female Eunuch* – read and reread since 1971 – and there, sure enough, in the first two pages is a tribute to Hazel Hunkins Hallinan, a woman who had spent her life working for women's liberation, who had watched the commitment to women's cause wax and wane throughout the twentieth century, and who was enthusiastic about the revival in spirit which the younger generation of women were bringing with them in 1970. 'Mrs Hazel Hunkins Hallinan, leader of the Six

Point Group', wrote Greer, 'welcomed the younger militants and even welcomed their sexual frankness. "They're young" she said . . . "and full of beans. The membership of our group until very recently has been too old for my liking" ' (Greer, 1970, p. 11).

This presented me with something of a puzzle. I would have been prepared to swear that I had had no prior knowledge of Hazel Hunkins Hallinan – or H[3] as she is so often called by her family and friends – and yet here I was confronting the indisputable evidence that I *had* heard of her – and on more than one occasion. In trying to make sense of this 'contradiction' I went back to something written by Blanche Wiesen Cook (1978), which seemed to strike a chord.

Cook has edited some of the writing of Crystal Eastman (a close friend of Hazel Hunkins Hallinan's), and in the Preface comments on the way that for years she 'knew' and 'yet did not know' about Crystal Eastman. Cook says that she was 'aware' of Eastman's existence but because of her culture and socialisation, her rules for making sense of the world, was 'programmed to deny' Eastman's contribution and significance (p. vi). With a sense of frustration Cook describes her activities as an historian studying World War I, concentrating as she did on the 'hard topics', (international diplomacy, foreign policy, etc.), so that when she was offered access to some of Crystal Eastman's papers of that time, she politely refused. Eastman just did not fit into the scheme of things, she just didn't seem relevant to any 'serious' study of that period.

Later, of course, Blanche Wiesen Cook, as a feminist and with a different consciousness and different perspective and priorities, was to become energised by Eastman's words and to place Eastman and her 'militant pacificism' at the centre of any understanding of World War I. She was also to confront the problem that I was experiencing of trying to explain why for so long she had put Eastman out of mind.

I find myself coming to the same conclusion as Blanche Wiesen Cook. Trained – or indoctrinated – as I had been to see any women's protest at the beginning of this century as a fleeting – and flighty – phase, as exhibitionism associated with gaining the vote, and as very peripheral to the fundamental and serious political issues, there was no room in my frame of reference to accommodate the significance of Hazel Hunkins Hallinan's seven decades of sustained support for women's interests. To have accepted that this woman was a feminist in 1913, was still a feminist in 1982, and had never wavered from her course or her convictions, would have been to undermine almost all of what I had been taught.

But like Blanche Wiesen Cook, I too have changed. Whereas a few years ago I may have 'ignored' the existence of Hazel Hunkins Hallinan in order to retain my conventional way of looking at the world, to keep my ideas that women have been *absent* from our cultural heritage, making their presence felt only on occasion and not often in a flattering light, I now choose to 'ignore' that conventional and patriarchal way of looking at the world so that I am free to appreciate and celebrate Hazel Hunkins Hallinan and her contribution to women. With no room in the conventional frame of reference to locate women like Crystal Eastman and Hazel Hunkins Hallinan (and Constance Rover, Dora Russell, Mary Stott and Rebecca West) then it is better to change the framework than to ignore these women and deny our traditions.

David Doughan, at the Fawcett Library, has challenged many of my assumptions about women's past and he also played a part in steering me towards my present understandings when he drew my attention to one of the more recent acquisitions of the Fawcett Library. It was the papers of the 'Six Point Group' donated by Hazel Hunkins Hallinan. 'You should know more about the "Six Point Group",' he said, 'And you certainly should know more about Hazel Hunkins Hallinan.' I took his advice and went through some of those fascinating documents – which also helped to re-educate me, and eliminated for ever from my consciousness the simplistic belief that middle-class and 'bourgeois' women were not interested in radical change – and I went to talk to Hazel Hunkins Hallinan.

She was ninety-one. She was sparkling, irreverent and immensely generous with her time, despite the fact that she was not in the best of health. As she talked about her life and her abiding interest in changing women's positions I became

increasingly aware of her significance, not just in terms of the
practical gains which she had helped make for women,
although these were and are undeniably important, but in
terms of her existence. She was a warm and sensitive woman
who was deeply offended and hurt by the unjust and cruel
practices of society and who from the best of motives and the
soundest of reasons had spent her life working to end such
abuses. She was proof of women's resistance, the evidence of
women's capacity to act, to contribute, to promote change, to
shape our society. She was a positive force. I am convinced
that she is representative of a multitude of women who, over
the centuries have worked to create a more humane and
reasonable culture, but whose existence the whole society
has been 'programmed to deny'.

Hazel Hunkins was born in Aspen, Colorado, USA on 6th
June 1890. Her mother, Ann Whittingham, had been born in
England and emigrated to America as a young child. Her
father, a Civil War veteran, Lewis Hunkins, was from
Massachusetts, and was a jeweller and watchmaker: he died
when she was thirteen, but this did not prevent her from
attending Vassar College, although in order to qualify she
had to go to Mt Ida school to remedy some of the defects of her
local education system. But early this century Hazel
Hunkins demonstrated a determination that is not all that
common among women today despite the twentieth century
'achievements': she wanted to be a scientist.

Her childhood, she says, in Billings, Montana, was as
happy as any child could wish and was crowned with four
glorious years at Vassar and then a wonderful job when she
graduated in 1913. For three years she taught at the
University of Missouri and began working on a Master's
Degree in chemistry (on the possible differences between
atomic weight of a lead extract and radio active rock),
immensely enjoying her work – and her independence. But
then her mother became ill and she was called home:
'Although my brother was at home it was the girl who was the
one who had to come home and take care of parents,' she said.
She gave up her job, and her research (which was never
completed) and returned to her home town.

'I was just stuck there,' she said; and there was nothing

she could do. There was temporary relief when she got a job in the local high school and thought she would be teaching science – but her hopes were quickly dashed when she found that was not to be.

'I had spent years being trained as a chemist. I had taken every chemistry course there was at Vassar and I thought I'd be able to teach chemistry. Then I discovered, "Oh no, we only have *men* teaching chemistry and physics – you will have to teach geography and botany." I knew nothing about botany. I knew nothing about geography. But that's what I had to teach. Only men had chemistry and physics – and so that was one of my first real blows about the limitations that were placed on women. It wasn't very tragic, but to a young girl it was tragic.' (Hunkins Hallinan, 1977)

Then came the summer, the summer of 1916: 'It was a summer of despair and unhappiness,' Hazel Hunkins Hallinan said, 'I was just waiting for time to pass.' At twenty-six, highly trained, wanting to work and do something worthwhile, wanting a purpose, and independence, she was forced into this passive and unpalatable existence. She had systematically written to every chemistry laboratory from one side of the United States to the other trying to obtain a job as an industrial chemist: her applications and correspondence were feet high. And she had for her efforts received over two hundred letters of rejection which simply stated 'We do not employ women as chemists.'

In her opinion many women come to understand the nature and extent of their oppression through their experiences in the workforce. Childhood, school, and even college *can* provide a relatively protected space where it is possible to rationalise that women are free to make their own choices and to stand or fall by their own efforts. But when confronted with blatant discrimination in employment this rationalisation can quickly disappear and women are obliged to face the fact that they are women and that their choices and opportunities are circumscribed – in the interest of men. It was the acknowledgment that she could not by her own efforts shape her own life and that this was the case for women in general that made a fervid feminist of Hazel Hunkins Hallinan.

During that dreary and demoralising summer a young woman, Anna Louise Rowe, came to Hazel Hunkins Hallinan's home town: 'She contacted the editor of the *Billings Gazette*, and he called me on the telephone and said there was a young lady in town from Washington, and he thought I would like to meet her. She had been sent to Montana by Alice Paul to organise the National Woman's Party, and for the first time in my life I heard the full philosophy of feminism described and explained to me. She got hold of me, and I fell for it hook, line and sinker. I was so ripe. I had spent so long smarting under those blows, feeling all those restrictions and rejections. Anna Louise Rowe offered me a chance to *do* something, not just for myself but also for all those other women who had been stopped like I had. And so it turned from a summer of despair into a summer of great happiness.'

Anna Louise Rowe's task was to organise branches of the National Woman's Party throughout the state and Alice Paul, the guiding force behind the party, was to become Hazel Hunkins Hallinan's life-long friend. At first H[3] began with organising a branch in Billings and then she went to the Colorado Convention of the newly formed National Woman's Party where they were organising its structure. It was exciting, and in more ways than one: it was here that she met Alice Paul and from then, there was no turning back!

Alice Paul was herself a very well-qualified woman who had graduated from Swarthmore College in 1905, become a social worker in New York, and had become disillusioned. She had gone to England where she studied in the Universities of Birmingham and London, and in the school of the militant suffragettes. A devout Quaker and pacifist she had become convinced of the absolute necessity of women's action and was gaoled once in Scotland and twice in England before returning to America to revitalise the suffrage movement. Along with Lucy Burns, Crystal Eastman and Mary Ritter Beard she had first formed the Congressional Union which was designed to put much the same pressure on the party in power in the US Congress, as the suffragettes were putting on the British Parliament.

The theory that it was the party in power which should be held responsible for failing to give women the vote was one that had not previously been used as a basis for action by the American suffrage movement. In Britain, the suffragettes had given up the 'pretence' of seeing themselves as 'members' of one political party or another and had labelled the entire system as the 'Men's Parliament' while they held their own meetings as the 'Women's Parliament' nearby: they had even gone so far as to insult and denature men's political differences by declaring that the political divisions among men were nothing other than men's 'personal problems' (see for example Teresa Billington-Greig, n.d.). Instead of dividing their efforts among the male parties or backing a particular party which in their estimation offered the best chance for women's suffrage (tactics which had for decades been pursued unsuccessfully), the suffragettes changed their strategies, put all men in the same boat, and concentrated their efforts on inconveniencing the party in power.

The Suffragette (20 December 1912) carried an 'Open Letter' on the front page in which it was calmly announced that from a practical point of view the anger and irritation of the politicians were very often more desirable than their approval:

> Your approval in the majority of cases leads to nothing. There are two ways of moving you to action. One is to stir your emotions by means of some appalling tragedy, dramatically described for you by the Press. The other is to make you thoroughly uncomfortable. The more effective of these two ways is to make you uncomfortable!

> Your sympathy and your emotion often fade away before anything has been done, whereas a continuing inconvenience, such as Suffragist militancy, never lets you rest until you have performed your duty. . . .

> You cannot expect the Suffragettes to give you a quiet life unless you in return will give them the Vote. . . .

> We have been very patient with you hitherto. Even now we feel no bitterness. When all is over we will give you a free pardon for your neglect of our interests and liberties. But

there can be no peace without honour – no end to fighting
till the Vote is won. – Yours for peace or for war,

The Suffragettes

In the main, these were the principles that won the
support of Alice Paul. There was no conflict with her pacifism
for the Suffragettes never committed acts of violence against
the person (although, of course, many were committed
against *them*, see Caroline Morrell, 1981), and conceived of
'militancy' as everything from asking questions at cabinet
ministers' public meetings to attacking men's property (and
when men showed themselves to be more concerned with
their pride and their property than with their self-appointed
role as woman's protector, the Suffragettes scored a valuable
point.) Dispensing with 'the theory of good conduct' (the
theory which had been the basis for suffrage strategies in
Britain for over fifty years) in favour of 'the theory of bad
conduct' and making men as uncomfortable as possible, had
much to recommend it. Alice Paul subscribed to it and the
San Francisco Convention of the National Woman's Party
(which grew out of the Congressional Union) decided to
practise it.

'The strategy was not particularly new, in the history of
US politics I suppose,' Hazel Hunkins Hallinan said in her
1977 talk to the Women's Press Club in Washington, 'but it
was the first time it had ever been applied so absolutely. We
were to hold the party in power responsible for acts of commission and omission. Now every party had its platform . . .
and they had the Women's Suffrage Amendment in their
platform, but as soon as the party was elected, well, the
amendment sank through the cracks in the platform and was
gone. It was never heard of again so it wasn't much good
getting the amendment into the party platforms.

'Alice Paul changed all that. She said "The Democratic
Party has been in power for four years – that was from 1912 –
1916 – and it hasn't done a thing about the suffrage amendment. We've been nagging them for four years and they have
done nothing, so we go into the 1916 election opposing the
Democratic Party."

'Well, of course all the "Democrat" women who belonged

to the National Woman's Party thought that was pretty terrible. They couldn't go against their own party, but it only took Alice Paul to convince them. And the National Woman's Party became an anti-Democratic Party, solely on the basis that they had been in power for four years and done nothing' (1977: 1982).[7]

The National Woman's Party started campaigning against the Democrats – and particularly against Wilson. Hazel Hunkins Hallinan can list numerous nuisance activities that were undertaken. There were demonstrations, meetings, public speeches and picket lines. When it came to getting a crowd together, she informed Jeannette Smyth in 1972, as a beginner, she used to be sent out first. She would start to make her speeches on women's rights until the single spectator had become a small crowd, and once the crowd grew to a reasonable size, a better speaker was sent in to take over. 'When they'd collected a really big crowd, they'd send out Mabel Vernon,' she told Smyth, 'She was one of the best.'

'That was the time that the war was going on in Europe and President Wilson was going around the country and doing a lot of talking about democracy, equality and freedom, and Alice Paul conceived the idea of throwing his words back at him. We had these enormous banners made with his words on them, but applying them to women. All those wonderful sayings of President Wilson's – like "Mr President, you say liberty is the fundamental demand of the human spirit – *How long must women wait?*", and "Freedom for everybody, *why not women?*" We must have made millionaires out of those banner-makers because we had new ones every day with all those marvellous sayings. You should go back to those speeches of Wilson's, they really were wonderful for us,' said Hazel Hunkins Hallinan, 'and he had to read them every time he came back home – when he rode in that automobile through those gates. He couldn't miss his own sayings which we were applying to women' (1977: 1982).

Joining the National Woman's Party meant joining the picket-line outside the White House in 1917 for Hazel Hunkins Hallinan, and this in many respects was no easy thing to do. It was not (and still is not) a matter of little consequence for a woman to dispense with approval and respectability: there is even an element of contradiction in women's decision to deliberately disrupt society and to promote confrontation, out of a desire for better social organisations based on co-operation and harmony. But it was not only their social acceptance that was at risk, it was also their physical safety.

It is misleading to refer to women's actions of that time as *militant*, states Hunkins Hallinan, because it has connotations of *violence* and violent was what the women were not! 'The protest was the least militant it could possibly be as far as we were concerned. Alice Paul was a devout Quaker. She didn't like violence. She didn't like "militancy" and there was nothing that any woman in the militant movement did which was militant. Militancy was *against* us, not by us,' she declared firmly in 1977. But as an 'afterthought' she added, 'I have to make one exception – it's not true, I may say – but I was accused of kicking a policewoman in the bosom and how I, at five feet one inch could manage to kick a policewoman in the bosom, I don't know. That is the only piece of "militancy" that ever was perpetrated – and it wasn't perpetrated!' (1977: 1982).

That women's actions – and women's political actions – are misrepresented is a 'fact' that Hazel Hunkins Hallinan has had to live with throughout her life. Less cynical than I am, she still expected reason and justice to prevail and was quite astonished that the peaceful and silent protest of women's picketing – and the hostility and violence of so many men – could have been 'reversed' in the popular consciousness. When I suggested that this was 'no accident', but that, on the contrary women's protests against male power were deliberately distorted in the attempt to demonstrate that there was 'something wrong with the women' and 'nothing wrong with male power or the men' she was quite disturbed by this particular interpretation. 'Surely not,' she said, and then added, 'But it does make sense. But that makes men even worse than I thought they were.'

She certainly didn't have a very high opinion of men in 1917 when she was on duty outside the White House. The violence against women was quite horrific – more noticeably after America entered the war and slogans on the pickets' banners announced the presence of 'Kaiser Wilson'.

Standing silently on picket duty was more than an endurance test: 'the crowds were very unfriendly. We used to grit our teeth for the insults. When the civil servants came out from work at 4.00 pm "Dirty bitches – what are you doing here?" they would shout. Sometimes it was even worse than that,' H[3] said to Marlene Cimons (1980a). The men in the street could become hostile and violent, and banners were torn from the pickets' hands and their clothes ripped from their backs. 'I had my shirt waist torn off me once,' stated Hazel Hunkins Hallinan. The police were in sympathy with the hostile crowd – not the pickets. 'The police would drag you off and throw you around if they felt like it. And their language was abusive too' (ibid.)

While willing to elaborate on the dedication of the women involved and ready to relate some of the more exciting and lively episodes, Hazel Hunkins Hallinan was nonetheless determined not to romanticise this period of women's history: it was often unrewarding, wearying and rough work. But the violent response of many men taught her a lesson she never forgot.

There were compensating moments of elation, however; there was the time when with the assistance of Lucy Burns's bent knee she hoisted herself over the White House fence and started a small bonfire on the lawn, scrambling back over before the guards came. 'We did it right under their noses,' she said, 'but it wasn't much good for publicity purposes because they didn't dare let it be known that their security was so inadequate.' And there was the constant joy of President Wilson's discomfort. 'I can remember how we used to line up on both sides of the exit of the White House,' she said to Jeannette Smyth in 1972, 'he would drive out in a top hat with his face like granite, ignoring us and our placards. He jolly well knew what was on them though. He was a terrible man really. Such duplicity in his handling of the suffrage amendment.'

And such duplicity in his handling of peace! As Blanche Wiesen Cook states, the 1916 election was a divisive one for feminist pacifists because there was 'Hughes who seemed to promise suffrage with war, or Wilson, who promised peace without suffrage' (p. 16). In the end, of course, they got Wilson, and no peace and no suffrage, but during the election campaign the differences between the two candidates led to different priorities among women, with some like Crystal Eastman devoting their energy to securing peace, with others putting their energy into the war effort, and Alice Paul and the National Woman's Party persisting with its campaign against President Wilson.

So, apart from the rejoicing over the Russian Revolution (rejoicing which she shared with her friend Crystal Eastman), the tiring work on the picket line went on for Hazel Hunkins Hallinan who saw no reason for supporting the war efforts. Instead she would heat bricks and take them to stand on, for her vigil in the cold. 'They didn't stay hot for very long,' she commented wryly 'but it was better than standing on ice and snow.'

There was mob violence the day the women's banners referred to 'free Russia' when women had been granted the vote after the overthrow of the czarist regime. From that time it was a regular occurrence with service men in uniform attacking the pickets along with the 'civilians'. On 22 June 1917 the first arrests were made.

The authorities found themselves in an awkward situation for 'the truth was that the women were violating no law, perpetrating no crime,' says Eleanor Flexner (1979), 'Their actions could only legally be classed as committing a nuisance,' but the punishment was by no means commensurate with the crime. 'At first the pickets were dismissed without sentence,' says Flexner, 'but as picketing and violence continued, the District courts began to sentence the women to jail, gradually increasing the term from a few days to six weeks and eventually to six months. A total of 218 women from 26 states were arrested during the first session of the Sixty-fifth Congress; 97 went to prison' (p. 295).

The conditions in the gaols – the Occoquan workhouse and the District of Columbia Gaol – were absolutely appalling, as Hazel Hunkins Hallinan well remembered. She was revolted and her family was scandalised, but she kept going back. 'When the women protested against the illegality of their arrests, the bad conditions, and the brutality of their treatment by going on hunger strikes,' states Flexner drily, 'the authorities, having learned nothing from the bitter experience of the British government, resorted to forced feeding and made martyrs wholesale' (p. 295). Men behaved much the same on both sides of the Atlantic, and this was an understanding Hazel Hunkins Hallinan retained throughout her life.

As in Britain, what little discussion has taken place on this aspect of women's history has usually concentrated on the efficacy or otherwise of militancy. Generally, there is little debate because in conventional terms there is no question that the *might* of the (male) state can triumph over the *might* of a few hundreds, or even a few thousands of women, and if *might* had been the issue, the British Suffragettes and the American National Woman's Party would have been the first to agree that there was *no contest*. But that was *not* the issue, regardless of the way it has been historically represented.

The issue was to embarrass, to expose the hypocrisy and duplicity of male political figures, and the National Woman's Party was no less successful in America in holding President Wilson up to scorn than were the Suffragettes in Britain who were holding Mr Asquith up to scorn. The 'militant' women who attacked male rationalisations helped to take away the sugar-coating and reveal the bitter nature of the pill. Freedom for 'everyone' – except women – whom men were pledged to represent: justice for 'all' – except women – who were illegally charged, convicted and assaulted; safety from attack and abuse for all 'persons' – except women – who were covered by male chivalry. It simply wasn't possible for anyone – no matter how well developed their tendencies for burying their heads in the sand – to ignore the blatant discrimination against women.

The Suffragettes and the National Woman's Party were completely successful in their aim of demonstrating that society was arranged in *men's* interest and that women did not have to put up with it: any discussions about whether or not militancy deprived women of respectability – or put back by years the battle for the vote – are just patriarchal distractions.

Partly because of her involvement with militancy, and partly because of the way she lived her life afterwards, Hazel Hunkins Hallinan has never subscribed to the belief that women are powerless. Talking about the Equal Rights Amendment in 1980 she said she was at a loss to understand why a well organised campaign would not result in ratification.

'Take the state of Illinois,' she said to Marlene Cimons (1980b), 'why don't we just go in there by the scores and picket the men who vote against it? Why don't we go to their meetings, interrupt them, picket – and vote against them?

'That's what we did in the 1916 election. We went into Missouri with a group of women from the suffrage states and concentrated on one congressman on the judiciary committee. We asked people to vote against him.'

And he was defeated. 'The word got around . . . it spread like wildfire that this old congressman had been defeated by the women. Every man in Congress got scared . . . It did us more good than anything else' (Cimons, 1982b).

Careful to avoid any hint of being patronising, and showing a remarkable capacity to listen – and to change her ideas – Hazel Hunkins Hallinan has asked, however, if women in today's women's movement might not learn something by studying the different style of the Suffragettes and the National Woman's Party. 'We made sure men had to think of *our* approval,' she said uncompromisingly, 'we weren't looking for theirs – and we didn't even have the vote at the time. Think what could be done if we could persuade women to *use* their vote collectively,' she said, and it was the only occasion on which I detected a note of regret in her voice, for in the Six Point Group which she joined not long after her arrival in England, she spent almost sixty years trying to get women to use their vote in their own interest.

After the war, and after the vote was won, Hazel Hunkins was contacted by the head of the research department of the American Railway Brotherhood and asked to undertake an assignment in England. The Railway Brotherhood wanted to find out all it could about the Co-operative

Movement in England, for there was no equivalent in the
United States, and the Brotherhood were well disposed
towards introducing such a movement. So in July 1920 she
arrived in England and made London her home until her
death in May, 1982.

It is usually suggested that she came not alone, and that
she accompanied her husband Charles Hallinan, the financial editor of United Press International. This is not accurate,
and as Hazel Hunkins Hallinan early and readily dispensed
with the cloak of respectability in favour of honesty and
integrity it seems in order to put the record straight. She
came alone, and with her own work to do: Charles Hallinan
came in November, with his own work to do. They lived
together: they had children. They were married, but at the
end of the 1920s and at the request of Hazel Hunkins's
mother and that of the children who wanted to have the same
name as their mother. This information comes on the best of
authority as does the statement, 'I have never in my life
called myself Mrs Charles Hallinan. I have always had my
own name.'

Hazel Hunkins found life in England very much to her
taste. Because of the nature of her assignment on the British
Co-operative Movement she was soon mixing within the
circle of political activists and theorists who made the
London School of Economics their focus. It was not long
before she wanted to study economics in a systematic way but
when she applied for entry to the London School of Economics
she soon found she wasn't a suitable candidate. 'They
wouldn't accept chemistry as an entry qualification,' she said
in a rather bemused tone, 'They told me I had to go back and
start from scratch. But they let me have a listening permit
and I was allowed to sit in on any lectures for £4.00 a term. It
was a lot of money, even then – and of course there were no
"qualifications" at the end – but that's how I got my training
in economics and politics' (1982)

During the 1920s and 1930s, Hazel Hunkins Hallinan
worked as a journalist – often for the *Chicago Tribune*[2] – and
acquired her own theoretical and practical knowledge of
politics and economics. She was among many of the radicals
of the time, being a frequent attender at the Fabian Socials –

where, incidentally, she met Beatrice Webb. The Fabian
Socials were one of the high points of her life: 'There were
conferences held regularly, and they were so interesting,' she
said. 'They would be held in a country house or a hotel, for a
week or weekend. Always there were these exciting and
stimulating speakers – and we would talk and talk and talk.
We discussed politics, and policies – and women – for hours
and hours. It was such a marvellous time and we were so
optimistic. Really, it was a sort of "think-tank" discussion
group of the Labour Party. We were going to bring about all
the great changes but without a bloody revolution. We
thought it possible,' she added on reflection, 'to change the
world. And it should be possible to do that without violence
and revolution' (1982).

During the 1920s she lived with Charles Hallinan in
Lincoln's Inn Fields, and Nancy, their first (of four) children
was born there. While motherhood – at least at this stage –
did not prevent Hazel Hunkins Hallinan from leading an
'active' life, the spiral staircase at Lincoln's Inn Fields,
nearly did. It was her most vivid memory of the period: 'It just
went round and round and up and up,' she said, 'and there
was so much to carry.'

This was also a period of optimism for women. American
women had the vote: *some* Englishwomen had it in 1918 (and
women were allowed to stand as parliamentary candidates
from 1918) and 1929 witnessed the first of the 'flapper voters'
(of whom Mary Stott speaks). Women were going to be able to
use their vote positively – or so the feminists of the age
believed.

With her close friend Crystal Eastman, Hazel Hunkins
Hallinan talked and talked about what women could, and
might do, in the political arena. Crystal Eastman had
married an Englishman – Walter Fuller – who was Charles
Hallinan's best friend, and in 1982, Walter Fuller's sisters,
Cynthia Dane and Rosalind Fuller were still among Hazel
Hunkins Hallinan's closest friends. Crystal Eastman made a
number of trips to England and lived near Hazel Hunkins
Hallinan when in London and they spent a great deal of time
together plotting the bloodless revolution. 'We had a lot in
common,' said Hazel Hunkins Hallinan in 1982, 'one thing

being that we had a shared antipathy to certain British ways.'

Both women had many a trenchant criticism to make of 'woman's role', particularly the 'married woman's role' (Crystal Eastman wrote an article 'Marriage Under Two Roofs', *Cosmopolitan*, December 1923, and argued that separate establishments was at least one way of ensuring that the wife was not obliged to do the housework for two adults). While anxious to 'intervene' in 'men's politics' these two women never lost sight of the equally important 'women's politics' which with or without women's suffrage, men were apt to ignore.

They both actively campaigned for birth control, and for legalised abortion. 'When I was young, in the reproductive age,' said Hazel Hunkins Hallinan, 'unwanted pregnancies were always a problem. The issue of birth control and legalised abortion was always an undercurrent in any meeting of women. Being pregnant, and not wanting to be, was something that was there all the time, but it wasn't often talked about in an "open" way. But women were constantly exchanging "private" information on what you could do about it. It's hard to say how dangerous it was. But it was a fear women always had' (1982).

'The issue of abortion has been so difficult, so emotional' she said, 'and it has gone on for so long.' She spoke of some of the problems which women faced earlier this century and made no attempt to conceal her anger at the way the male controlled medical and legal professions had taken over abortion and were in an area where they had no right to be! 'It isn't a medical or legal matter,' she stated, 'it's a woman's matter. It's a case where you see men at their worst.'

She gave some examples. 'When I was young, if you went to a doctor you really knew, and said you were pregnant but you didn't want to be, then as a favour he might give you some "advice" and at the same time he'd disclaim any responsibility. He could know a *safe* way of carrying out an abortion, but because of the legal and medical entanglements you wouldn't get that. Instead, as a favour, you might get some very *unsafe* advice. Like "go home and take aspros till your ears ring". That's the sort of ridiculous thing that happens when the male doctors and lawyers get involved. It's not the women they think of, but their own rules and regulations. If you asked a doctor to help you, he'd raise his hands and say "I have to think of my career". They didn't worry much about women's careers. Fancy, doctors in the name of their profession and as a favour to some of their women patients giving unsafe advice to women on a matter they shouldn't be meddling in anyway. That's why it's a woman's issue,' she insisted.

I told her of some of the more recent developments in the United States where women were very definitely taking matters into their own hands. Pauline Bart (1981) has written of the need for women to 'seize the means of reproduction' and has described the activities of an 'illegal' feminist abortion clinic, discussing how and why it worked. 'It appeals to me,' I said, 'to think of men sitting round and making up the rules while the women continue to show that the rules have nothing to do with women's reproduction.'

'I thoroughly approve,' said Hazel Hunkins Hallinan. 'They call it barbaric times before doctors came on the scene, but it was a time when women took care of their own. It's much more barbaric now . . . and we still have to keep marching and demonstrating to protect what we have got. There'll be another man in parliament shortly who will bring in another anti-abortion bill, look what's going on in the States.' She was quiet for a while and then smiled broadly, 'Tell me more about this "illegal" feminist clinic,' she said.

In Hazel Hunkins Hallinan's mind there was no doubt that men have tried to control women through controlling reproduction. 'You couldn't make any mistakes about that when we were fighting for the legalisation of birth control information,' she declared. 'So many men didn't want women to know how to control the number of children they had. The men were quite disgraceful, and they were very threatened. They thought they'd lose control over women if women could refuse to have children.'

She corrected me when I said things had not changed much. 'Oh, but they have!' she said, 'You can't imagine what it was like when men would accept no responsibility for birth control, when they insisted that it was natural that women should keep on having children one after another. You can't imagine what it was like when we would get all worked up over the injustice of it – when we knew there was a way to stop it but they wouldn't tell us what it was, or how it worked, – and they would just shrug and say it was women's lot.'

'What women knew about themselves then was so different too,' she added, 'Women could only know about themselves through their husbands then. There was no other source of information. Today,' she said, 'you know things about yourself as women, you take it for granted. It would have horrified people in my day.' There have been 'improvements' even if the problem of male power remains much the same.

Marie Stopes she knew, and went to see, and while Hazel Hunkins Hallinan had much admiration for Stopes's work related to birth control, she thought that Marie Stopes had been a bit sentimental about the whole issue, glossing over the 'politics' with a veneer of 'married love'. Hazel Hunkins Hallinan had no such reservations about Dora Russell, however, another woman very involved in the birth control campaign. 'We were friends,' said Hazel Hunkins Hallinan 'and Dora lived nearby. I haven't seen her for years. But we used to see a lot of each other. I think she used to have a hard time on occasions because Bertrand Russell wouldn't let anything or anyone interfere with his philosophy.'

Another friend was Vera Brittain: 'She changed a lot with the birth of her daughter' said H[3], and with a twinkle, 'She got to be so proud of Shirley Williams, she stopped being proud of herself. It was a shame,' she said, 'she was a nice woman and worked so hard for women's issues – although she didn't want a bloody revolution either' (1982).

In the twenties there were many issues which had to be fought for, and there was a firm faith that much was going to be achieved. Hazel Hunkins Hallinan was a member of the '1917 Club,' which as its title suggests was comprised of people who supported the aims and aspirations of the Russian Revolution. The 1917 Club, with its headquarters in 4 Gerard Street ('an address etched firmly in my memory,' declared H[3], who was sometimes apologetic about dates and places which she had forgotten), met regularly for luncheon meetings, and was a gathering place for all the revolutionaries of the time. 'I can't remember whether Jack Reed[3] ever came,' she said, 'he was a good friend. But,' she added rather twinklingly, 'I was one of the women he *didn't* sleep with!'

I asked Hazel Hunkins Hallinan what had been the most important event in her life in the twenties and the answer came back without hesitation: 'Joining the Six Point Group was the most important thing I ever did,' she declared.

In 1921 the Six Point Group was established by Margaret Haig (Viscountess Rhondda), a *very* successful businesswoman. She had played an active part in the battle to obtain the vote for women (she had been a member of the WSPU and gone to gaol for her efforts) and she was determined to play an active part in the battle for women to use their votes responsibly. To this end she had funded the feminist magazine, *Time and Tide*[4] in 1920, which was to be a women's journal of political discussion and debate – it was to support women politicians of all parties, evaluate policies from women's point of view, and monitor the behaviour of male politicians – and to this end she also founded the discussion and pressure group, the Six Point Group.

The name came from the six points that were considered necessary in the interests of women's equality. In 1923, in a supplement to *Time and Tide* written by Elizabeth Robins, the 'six points' were clearly set out. Over the years some of the points were achieved – such as the end to the marriage-bar for women in the Civil Service – but some remain as relevant today as they did sixty years ago – for example, equal pay and equality of opportunity in the workforce were among the original six demands. But if and when one particular problem was removed, it was immediately replaced by another demand. 'You could just go on and on,' said Hazel Hunkins Hallinan, 'adding more points to work for.' When interviewed in 1969 for *She*, by Marjorie Barrett, Hazel Hunkins Hallinan – then seventy-nine years of age – declared that 'The fight is on until we have full economic, legal, occupational, moral, social and political equality.' These were the six points still being fought for when the Six Point Group was disbanded by its last president, Hazel Hunkins Hallinan, in 1981.

Obviously, it was no easy task for her to call an end to the sixty-year-old organisation and while she expressed many regrets about its demise, it was a step that had to be taken. For no younger women joined to swell the ranks.

We had a long discussion about the 'failure' of modern feminists to involve themselves in 'mainstream' politicking. Hazel Hunkins Hallinan had spent sixty years of her life 'fighting behind the government scene' as she called it: she had tirelessly worked for and achieved many of the legal and political reforms which I take for granted – and perhaps which, if removed, would send me into the mainstream of politics to agitate for their restoration. Much of her energy had gone into the Sex Discrimination Act, and the Equal Pay Act, and she knew their limitations better than I did. In her terms there was still a lot to be done on the parliamentary front but there were few young women prepared to take up the challenge.

It would have been possible for me to argue that the Houses of Parliament were not the places where women procure the changes they wanted. I did suggest that when women became political partners men had not exactly seen it as a reason for becoming domestic partners: women hadn't been able to use the vote to get men to do the housework, accept responsibility for child-rearing, or even to protect themselves from male violence at home or in the street. Hazel Hunkins Hallinan completely agreed, and made it quite clear that there were limitations on what women could do with their legal and political rights: but she also insisted that women were not making full use of the legal and political rights they possessed and that because of this, the Six Point Group, and *Time and Tide* were needed no less today than they had been in the 1920s. And I had to agree.

'Of course, the milieu is different today,' she said, 'of course, different generations have different values, different priorities, and different styles. But in the way feminists have turned away from the law and politics as a means of bringing about change, don't you think they might be running the risk of throwing the baby out with the bathwater?'

It was a 'sensitive' issue for both of us. It was not beyond the realms of my imagination to visualise settings in which

Hazel Hunkins Hallinan's long and tested commitment to parliamentary reform could have been 'dismissed' by contemporaries who are reaping the rewards of those reforms. I could not, however, share her faith in the political processes: as with institutionalised education, I think institutionalised politics has been set up by men and is controlled by men and that it is misguided to expect that from within the bastion of male power will come the reforms aimed at ending that power.

Hazel Hunkins Hallinan argued that women could and should use their political strength to stop male violence against women. She was full of admiration for the grass-roots protests against pornography, for the demonstrations to 'reclaim the night', but she remained convinced that all this energy was being dissipated because there was no channel from it to 'behind the scenes' where the pressure was applied. 'The few women Members of Parliament who count themselves as feminists are under enormous strain,' she said, 'for there isn't the back-up that there used to be for women like Edith Summerskill.'

There was no doubt that she was at a loss to explain why strategies which had worked so well in her own time were dismissed out of hand today. Recognising that it wasn't 'fashionable' to hold up the example of individual women she nonetheless wanted it to be on record that there *have* been individual women with particular skills who have been worth their weight in gold in the women's movement. 'Take Inez Mulholland,' she said, 'she was a superb speaker and diplomat. She was a striking woman who could sway an audience. When there was an audience that needed swaying, she got called in. No one thought any the more or the less of her because she had such skills. But we were all ready to admit that she had them – and to use them when they were needed.'

'And Alice Paul. She really could galvanise women into action. She was the force behind the National Woman's Party. There wouldn't have been any National Woman's Party without her.' The questions went unasked, but they were there: at the risk of being branded a heretic, I cannot help but wonder whether we need popular images to organise around, and whether we are denying the skills of some women. Hazel Hunkins Hallinan didn't have any doubts: one of the reasons she saw for the success of the anti-ERA movement and the anti-choice movement in the United States was because they were organised around specific women. She felt a considerable amount of frustration at being denied media feminists in a media-saturated age. 'The only people who profit from this arrangement are non-feminists,' she said firmly.

She gave me much to think about, but much to amuse me too.

"Margaret Thatcher is a remarkable woman – and please don't take that as any comment on her party politics or policies,' she quickly added. 'I knew her when she was just out of Oxford and she used to go all round the countryside, making speeches everywhere. I'm very disappointed in her policies, but just the same, she is remarkable. She's a bit of a nuisance though, because she's always the exception that men quote when they are trying to ruin your case.'

'When she was much younger she came to give a speech at the Six Point Group. She was an excellent speaker. She knew what rights women didn't have. She was always being given "advice" about her political career by men. There was one man – I won't mention his name – who told her to go home and have her family first – and then come back into politics. It was characteristic of her to go home and have twins. She was always very determined,' (1982)

'Men are always giving women advice about their jobs, and their lives,' H[3] said satirically, 'but I've never heard a man tell a woman to get herself a good wife. But it's what they've got, and take for granted. They even think they should get the credit for being well organised and efficient when all the time it is their wives who are responsible.'

'Do you think parliamentary reform would be helpful?' I asked, unable to let the opportunity pass, and feeling a bit ungracious even as I spoke. 'Of course not,' she answered with a smile. 'But you could have parliamentary reforms to make sure the job of politician is open to women. It isn't at the moment. Women have to choose between family and work as it is arranged now. I'd like to see the 300 Club[5] getting more support.'

As far as H[3] was concerned, there should be a network of women – everywhere. Despite the fact that many of us today may think we 'invented' networking, women's networks functioned and flourished earlier this century according to Hazel Hunkins Hallinan. To her, one of the greatest wastes was the way that network had not recruited new members. There had been no continuity, no links between one generation and the next: 'It just seemed to die out,' she said 'literally!'

For the last few years she had found herself very much alone, with captions in newspapers heralding her as the last surviving Suffragette, and making comments on her 'faculties' in the face of advancing age. This she did not find flattering. But there were some aspects of aging that she found quite amusing.

When her husband died in 1971 she took his ashes to Billings to bury beside her parents. As the memorial stones on her parents' graves had deteriorated she decided to have four new ones made – including her own – which she asked the stone mason to keep until it was needed. Later, she returned to Billings and rang an old friend. 'Hazel? Good heavens,' her friend said, 'I thought you were dead. I saw your tombstone in the cemetery.'

Death had seemed a lot closer at times during the World War 2, than it did in 1982, she informed me. At the start of the war she was made an air raid warden and had the job of patrolling the streets in her area: 'There had to be a complete blackout,' she said, 'there was to be no light anywhere. If you saw the faintest crack of light showing through the curtains you had to knock the people up and tell them.'

'I was out doing that one night when a bomb came over. You could hear them coming. There was a change in the noise level and you knew that meant the bomb was coming. It was right above me, and there was nothing I could do. We were taught to lie in the gutter – in the curb where the dogs go – Ugh!' she said with obviously vivid recollections. 'And so I got down, and put my head on my hands, because the bomb raises your head and otherwise you'd bang it on the pavement,' she added by way of explanation. 'I flattened myself out and it came down on the other side of the street. Number 35 was destroyed and Number 33 and 37 were gutted. And the air was just like soup. It was awful with those houses just blasted to smithereens. My lungs got blasted, and I breathed in all that rotten air. I was in hospital for eleven months – first of all in Hampstead and then at Bognor Regis. It was depressing and demoralising,' she said. 'I was there on my own all the time.'

Two of her children, Joyce and Mark, remained in London at first, but after the Blitz, they were sent off to New York. During the later war years Hazel Hunkins Hallinan worked on the committee which evacuated British children to the United States.

In the fifties the battle for women's rights went on. H[3] showed me some of the press clippings from this period and had no difficulty in convincing me that there have been some improvements.

One was from *The Daily Mirror* (25 September 1950) and was enough to make the blood of the most sanguine woman boil:

ROVING EYE HUSBANDS MUST NEVER BE 'FOUND OUT' WOMEN ARE TOLD
The husband who has a 'roving eye' is only acting true to his nature – and a wife should make allowances for it, a psychologist told a women's meeting yesterday. *But the husband should also understand, he added, that he must never disillusion his wife about his faithfulness. He must never be found out.*

Dr Eustace Chesser, secretary of the Society for Sex Education and Guidance was speaking to twenty-five women members of the Six Point Group at Leatherhead, Surrey. He said 'Man is promiscuous by imagination or instinct, a 'roving eye' is part of his nature.'

He urged women to believe that there is a great deal of the child in a man, and a wife should in a sense, be a mother to her husband as well as her child.

First to challenge Dr Chesser was middle-aged Mrs Hunkins Hallinan, who said:-

'If a husband is unfaithful and the wife makes allowances, perhaps six months later he'll be unfaithful again. Is the wife to treat her man as an infant all his life?'

Dr Chesser replied: 'All I am saying is that this roving eye is part of man's makeup. But I don't say he should be encouraged or allowed to indulge it.' (my emphasis)

A blatant and convenient double standard and one that Hazel Hunkins Hallinan had no time for. But it was everywhere in the fifties and helped to ensure that the middle-aged, 'embittered' and undoubtedly unhappy women of the Six Point Group were treated as 'out of their time'. In her long life H[3] experienced many periods when her feminism was seen as unfashionable. It did not deter her from practising it. And the Six Point Group was always a basis for support.

In March 1958, at a meeting of the Married Women's Association (of which Vera Brittain was the president) Hazel Hunkins Hallinan reported on her recent visit to Russia (she seems to have refrained from mentioning the fact that she had placed a bouquet of flowers on Jack Reed's grave when she visited the Kremlin). From the minutes of the meeting it appears that she received a positive response – and she certainly gave a positive account of many features of Russian life as they related to women. She had praise for the creches and for the system of divorce (and property settlement), although if the minutes of the meeting are any guide she must have expressed some apprehension about the Russian rationalisation for the eradication of prostitution: 'Prostitution is a business based on immorality and the Russians claim that since they have removed the economic incentive, the business has collapsed. They will not tolerate any organisation or "entrepreneur" whose profit is derived in this way.'

'We had great hopes of the Russian Revolution in 1917,' she said, 'we had an enormous celebration when we found out that the czarist regime had been overthrown. But somehow, the idealism went out of the revolution – or at least, it did for us,' she added. 'You can't speak for the Russians. You can't make judgments on their behalf. The Russian character is so different, their traditions are so different that you can't say it hasn't been what they hoped for. But for those of us who were revolutionaries it was possible to hang on to our illusions for only a short while. It wasn't the revolution *we* wanted. I was very disillusioned by the way Alexandra Kollontai was treated – I couldn't feel the same way about the revolution after she was exiled as ambassador to Sweden.'[6]

A disillusioned person Hazel Hunkins Hallinan certainly was not, though there had been many occasions in her many years where her hope of a soon-to-be-realised equality had to give way to the recognition that women's liberation was to be a long, hard struggle. It even had to be admitted that partial gains in one area could often be offset by the introduction of yet more new obstacles. But still, she was unwavering in her belief that improvements had been made.

In 1968 she had edited a book, a discussion document of the Six Point Group (*In Her Own Right*) in which she commented on the changes that had occurred for women over the century. It was noticeable, she said, that in the main such changes 'involved the removal of specific disabilities written into the law' and each change followed 'a hard fought campaign' (which she had generally been involved in). 'The limited aspect of these freedoms established a facade of equality behind which hide all the other disabilities and barriers women resent. It is behind this facade that the problems of the next fifty years lie;' (p. 14). This was almost fifty years *after* the Six Point Group had been formed, and it was *before* Hazel Hunkins Hallinan knew that there would be a revitalisation of the women's movement. She was aware that much more needed to be done – but she was equally insistent that much had been achieved.

It was the possibility of an Equal Pay Act and a Sex Discrimination Act – as well as the establishment of an Equal Opportunities Commission – that commanded her attention. With each of these she admitted that she had believed they would bring about great changes, and had been disappointed. But that was no reason to give up the fight as far as she was concerned.

She talked of the great hopes that women allowed

themselves to have, only to find that the legislation they had worked for had 'loopholes' which they could not possibly have foreseen. She quoted the more recent example of the Equal Pay Act. After years of lobbying 'behind the scene' it was brought in by Barbara Castle – 'one of the finest politicians the world has ever produced' (1977) – and women, understandably, had great expectations of tangible progress.

'Barbara Castle got that law through an unwilling parliament, an unwilling press and an unwilling trade union movement in 1970, and it came into effect in 1975. And we thought women would start to get the same pay as men for the same work. But we hadn't bargained on how it could be wilfully misinterpreted,' she added.

'After the Equal Pay Act, I went through a shoe factory where they were making men's shoes and women's shoes. There were a lot of women pounding shoes – putting heels on actually. And there were a lot of men in another part putting heels on shoes. I said to the manager "I suppose you have equal pay?" And he said "Oh yes, we have equal pay." So I asked him, "Do you mean to say that the women here running this machine and the men over there running the same machine, get the same pay?" He said "Oh no! Heavens no! Those men are putting heels on *male* shoes. The women are putting heels on *women's* shoes. It's not the same work."

'There were six nails going into each shoe,' Hazel Hunkins Hallinan declared 'and they were using the same machines. But the women didn't get the same pay' (1977: 1982).

She needed no reminder that men 'called the shots', that they defined the terms and could quickly change them to suit their own convenience – a common practice when women looked like making inroads into territory men had reserved for themselves. But even women could be forgiven for failing to anticipate that the Equal Pay Act could be implemented in this way. It took a peculiar twist in logic (and a commitment to underpaying women) to arrive at this arrangement.

What could be anticipated as far as H[3] was concerned was the effort many men would make to undermine women's achievements. From the outset, she said, they declared that the Equal Pay Act wouldn't work and that the Equal

Opportunities Commission (EOC) would fail – and they then proceeded to ensure that their predictions came true.

'There are people criticising the EOC, saying that it's not a success, that it's no good, that it's failed,' she said, 'but what you don't hear is how this in itself makes difficulties, for it demoralises the people working for it: what you don't hear either is that parliament sabotaged it. When it came into being it was only given five million pounds for five years. That's only a million pounds a year. You can't *do* anything on a million pounds a year — I could, but the government can't. So the government really sabotaged it at its birth, by making money so short. The EOC has to employ lawyers to do its work, and lawyers cost money. And they simply haven't got the money to pay them' (1977).

'Men have always got so many "good reasons" for keeping their privileges,' she said exasperatedly. 'If we had left it to the men *toilets* would have been the greatest obstacle to human progress. *Toilets* was always the reason women couldn't become engineers, or pilots, or even members of parliament. They didn't have women's toilets.' We talked of the problem that plagued the Houses of Parliament after women were admitted (with toilets that were marked 'Members Only') and of the way toilets had been an issue raised against the passing of the Equal Rights Amendment in the USA (where some were frightened that it would be unconstitutional to have separate toilets for the sexes if the amendment were passed). How was it, we wondered, that so much silliness could ever be seen as 'sensible' while the good sense of so many feminists could often be seen as silly?

There had been so much nonsense about the Equal Rights Amendment and so many fears were played upon to prevent it from being ratified, but to Hazel Hunkins Hallinan the force of the opposition was an indication of the changes that the Amendment could accomplish. 'If they didn't think it would bring improvements, if they really thought it would fail,' she declared, 'they wouldn't be working so damned hard to stop it!' (1982).

Despite her sixty years in London, H[3] felt a particular bond with the Equal Rights Amendment: it was formulated by her close friend and fellow campaigner Alice Paul – who had built on the wisdom of Susan B. Anthony. For Hazel Hunkins Hallinan, having the ERA passed had been a goal for almost her entire adult life, and a goal that she was acutely conscious had not been achieved when she returned to Washington in 1977 to deliver the address at the Memorial Service for Alice Paul.

'Alice Paul,' she had said, 'made women's position a burning political issue. Women came from all over the country to take part in the demonstrations and pickets. They came and were attacked by mobs and clubbed by police; and they kept on coming!'

'You may well wonder how one young woman, slender, frail, modest, even shy, could manage all this,' she said, aware that so many of us believe that power lies in institutions and with the men who run them. But there is the power of women, and the power of justice, and Alice Paul had both of these: 'Within her spirit was a flame forcing her to make right what she thought to be wrong to her sex, and she communicated this in full strength to others.'

'Alice Paul had always known that "Votes for Women" would not protect them from discrimination,' which was why she drafted, and fought for the ERA. 'It would be the means of opening all the doors that are closed to women – innumerable doors closed by state laws, by custom, by history, by prejudice.'

Conscious of the way other women had devoted their lives to improving the position of their sex, Hazel Hunkins Hallinan concluded her address in commemoration of her friend: 'As Susan B. Anthony worked all her life for the suffrage amendment and died before it was realised, so Alice Paul worked all her life and died before her work reached fruition. Her name will go down in history as a woman working for the betterment of all women for all times – and in her honour we should dedicate ourselves anew to finishing our own liberation!' (1977b).

Hazel Hunkins Hallinan had a deep sense of women's history and an understanding that she was part of an old and honoured tradition. When she became part of the women's movement in 1917 it was in the knowledge that she was the inheritor of a tradition of a long line of women who had for decades been working for women. She was in 1917, one of the new, young members entrusted with the task of continuing the struggle, and this she did for more than sixty years. Hence her sense of astonishment that it could be widely believed that there was something *new* about women's determination for liberation.

'It wasn't even *new* at the beginning of the century,' she said, 'and its been going on all *through* this century.' In her eyes there was an unbroken line right back at least as far as 1848 and Seneca Falls when Elizabeth Cady Stanton and Lucretia Mott – among others – had put forward the declaration of women's rights. 'It still hasn't been put into practice,' said Hazel Hunkins Hallinan, 'They would never have believed it would take so long' (1982).

And the passing of time brought with it its own problems: every generation has had to provide recruits. Again and again women have had to dedicate themselves anew to ensuring women's liberation.

For Hazel Hunkins Hallinan there was the deeply disturbing question of why women didn't get together – once and for all – and put an end to the issue. 'We do have such power, and we don't use it,' she said, and she wasn't referring simply to the ballot box, although she was certainly including it. 'Women *can* change society and I simply don't understand why we aren't raising hell. We should be out there being so outrageous and causing such a nuisance, that it would be easier for men to settle with us. Why don't we do it?' she asked me.

She was genuinely puzzled that so many women could not see the necessity of joining the women's movement.[7] We talked about the 'bad press' that those in the women's movement generally received, where they used to be labelled as unsexed, hysterical spinsters but are now more likely to warrant epithets such as castrating, embittered and humourless; but not even such a 'bad press' could be responsible for discouraging some of the women who went out of their way to condemn a movement that was in their own interest.

H[3] talked of the terrible trap of 'self sacrifice' whereby women were asked to believe that it was better to work for others, rather than themselves. And we talked about economic (and emotional) dependence and the understandable reluctance to 'bite the hand that feeds you'. But still the question remained. 'Perhaps,' she said, with optimism, 'this is really the *last* hurdle. Perhaps it is the power that men have over women's minds that is the final and most elusive barrier to be broken.'

She said that she felt more confident of success in 1982 than she had in 1968 when she had written: 'The great crusading spirit for equality which was so strong at the turn of the century has petered out and the most dramatic revolution of all times has never been brought to fruition' 1968 (p. 9). 'That,' she said with some amusement,' was before you younger women came along. That was before I knew you would take over from us, as we had taken over from those who had fought for suffrage. Your methods might be a bit different, but then so were ours. I *feel* a lot more optimistic now' (1982).

But if today's methods are different, the aims are much the same. The purpose of *In Her Own Right* in 1968 was 'to open the eyes of teenage girls starting out in life . . . so that they will demand a better chance; to persuade newly married wives not to abdicate their rights as people to an unequal partnership in marriage; to reach those older women who have shied away from "women's movements" and who learn late in life what odds are stacked against them. We want to make these thousands realize what their actual status is and then we hope that the emancipation of women, as a movement, will come alive' (p. 10).

Hazel Hunkins Hallinan felt gratified that the emancipation of women as a movement *had* come alive. Because of the revitalisation of the women's movement she thought that some of her statements in *In Her Own Right* were no longer relevant. But there were some she saw no need to change.

'Generation after generation of little girls have become adults completely conditioned to an overwhelming masculine society,' she had written, and this restricted 'the development of women, until they have no vision of anything different before them' (1968, p. 9). 'This is still where it is at today,' she said.

All her adult, feminist life, Hazel Hunkins Hallinan was

conscious that she was part of a tradition of reasonable and responsible women who had a vision of social justice. In 1968 when she called for women's liberation she had said, 'No new ideas these! They were first mooted in England by Mary Wollstonecraft in 1792,[8] and were discussed ... as a philosophy of freedom so comprehensive that some of its concepts are too far reaching for feminists today' (p. 11). I hope that this is one of the statements that she would have chosen to change: Hazel Hunkins Hallinan has given us much to live up to.

Chapter 2

REBECCA WEST
Born 1892

> I am an old fashioned feminist. I believe in the sex war.
> When those of our army whose voices are likely to coo tell
> us that the day of sex antagonism is over and that
> henceforth we only have to advance hand in hand with the
> male, I do not believe it.

When I first read some of Rebecca West's articles written
early this century, *I* couldn't believe it. I simply did not know
that women had written so daringly and defiantly and in such
a spirit of joy and celebration. I didn't know that in times past
– times I had been taught to see as but a preliminary for
today's 'bold' venture – women had dropped so deliberately
their deference for men and had engaged in such frank and
guiltless analysis, criticism and mockery of men – and survived! Or survived in a sense: that I thought we were the first
generation to do away with the pretence that 'what every
woman needs is a man', and to start describing and explaining male behaviour in *our* terms rather than *theirs*, helps to
indicate how women's words of protest do not survive. 'Men
are such poor stuff,' said Rebecca West, repeatedly, in 1913,
and seventy years later she didn't see much reason for
changing her mind.

   'We have asked men for votes, they have given us advice,'
she wrote in *The Clarion* (18 April 1913), and 'At present they
are also giving us abuse. I am tired of this running comment
on the war-like conduct of my sex, delivered with such
insolent assurance and such self-satisfaction. So I am going
to do it too,' and with enthusiasm and alacrity she begins her
denunciation, 'Men are poor stuff' (ibid.).

   'Men are very poor stuff,' she goes on to exclaim after she
has described the way the editor of the *Pall Mall Gazette* is
encouraging the public to lynch the suffragettes; 'Oh, men
are very poor stuff indeed,' she declares as she traces the
history of male politicians' deception and cruelty; 'Oh, men
are miserably poor stuff!' she concludes when she gives an
account of the judge's tantrums and tyranny at the trial of

Mrs Pankhurst. Uncompromisingly, unflinchingly and un-
failingly she itemised the self-interested nature of male
behaviour and reasoning, refusing to comply with the form
thought proper to the female sex: in the process she drew the
battle-lines of the sexes.

It is her irreverence which was striking then and which
is still apparent today. Rebecca West makes it clear that we
have taken the enemy too seriously: he has given himself airs
and graces, has insisted on his authority, and has expected to
be treated with respect, and all his efforts may come to
nothing when instead of being impressed we are overcome
with mirth by the ridiculousness of his posture. This touch of
hers – which is nothing less than brilliant, although one can
appreciate why it is that men have not seen fit to describe it in
this way – is revealed again and again as in her late teens and
early twenties she tackled the 'intellectual giants' of her day,
unfalteringly found the flaws and paraded them on the public
stage.

One such 'victim' was Sir Almroth Wright who revealed
his intellectual stature in a letter he wrote to *The Times*
against women's suffrage (and which being 'news' of course,
The Times dutifully printed on its front page as it conducted
its cautious and concerned campaign against votes for
women), as well as in his book the *Unexpurgated Case
Against Woman Suffrage*. 'I feel joyously confident of the
female wits,' wrote West upon reading Wright's book for 'It is
the worst book ever written,' and in her barbed and bold way
she goes on to criticise the writer's style: 'I have horrible
nightmares of Sir Almroth Wright's limp sentences wander-
ing through the arid desert of his mind looking for dropped
punctuation marks. They have a brooding look in their eyes
like childless women, for every sentence ought to have a little
meaning clasped in its arms, but these have none' (*The
Clarion*, 17 October 1913). What Wright meant – in deadly
earnestness – West finds uproariously funny.

'This book is the tragedy of my life,' she complains, for
'Months ago when it was announced by the publishers I
promised myself the joy of tearing it limb from limb. And now
it has no limbs – only two rudimentary organs embedded in a
mass of protoplasmic jelly.' There is no mistaking her

disappointment that this particular intellectual giant cannot put up a good show: West indicates that she feels quite cheated as she describes the poor case that Wright has put forward. His first point is that woman should not have the vote because she is an insolvent citizen and does not earn her keep, to which West retorts that this 'motherhood is an extravagant hobby of hers which she carries on simply to give trouble.' And his second point 'is a belief in the imbecility and immorality of women. "There are no good women," ' he says, ' "only women who have lived under the influence of good men." ' To Rebecca West this statement is extraordinary (a term she is still fond of today when she describes the limitations of male logic), but it is not the only time that the worthy gentleman and unworthy opponent 'lapses into comedy' for he also declares in all seriousness that spinsters are of retarded development, that the absence of a man in their life is an intellectual liability, and that examples of this can be found on county councils. 'I glory in the idea of Sir Almroth Wright's ghost explaining matters to the startled and dismayed members of the Women's Local Government Board Society,' West quips in conclusion (ibid.).

Coming to Rebecca West's feminist writings, after ten years of what I now sometimes see as tentative steps, has been for me a revelation. It is not just that I find her words of the last seventy years entertaining, enjoyable and inspiring but that they are in a sense symbolic; they represent a form of *permission*. They show me that it is all right to abandon the male-approval-device (MAD) that has been so carefully cultivated within us as women, and assure me that it is not only permissible but reasonable and responsible to register a protest against patriarchy – and to defy the consequences! When her words are such a powerful prompt to protest one can understand why efforts have been made to discredit them.

Of course the climate of the time helped to encourage and facilitate the stand which Rebecca West adopted at such an early age. The Women's Social and Political Union (WSPU) had been formed in 1903 (and Rebecca West had become a member during her teens) and the suffragettes shared a philosophy that was similar to the one expressed by Rebecca

West. Fundamental to militancy among women was the premise that women had to break out of the strait-jacket of politeness and passivity that had been imposed upon them, and Teresa Billington-Greig, for example, gave a good account of the necessity for women to stop reacting to men and to start initiating actions of their own when she declared that it was essential in woman's quest for independence that they demonstrated that they were a force to be reckoned with. It was crucial, Billington-Greig argued, that women be seen to challenge *all* facets of male authority for it was difficult for men to persist with their assertion that women were by nature passive and polite when women from all walks of life were daily demonstrating their (natural) capacity for resistance and rudeness. Men have used a 'theory of good conduct', said Billington-Greig (n.d.) in their attempt to disarm us, and have tried to persuade us that if we are retiring and respectful they will give us our rights. But this is just a trick, claimed Billington-Greig, for if we are good as they urge us to be, we are no trouble to them at all and there is absolutely no reason they should not ignore us, and refrain from granting us our rights!

Christabel Pankhurst who guided the strategy of the WSPU shared much the same analysis: men would listen to what women had to say only when they were forced to, she declared, and not before. Women would gain their rights only when men were uneasy about withholding them any longer and it was therefore women's task to make men terribly uneasy (see Dale Spender 1982b, and Elizabeth Sarah 1983 for further discussion). Obviously Rebecca West had reached a comparable conclusion and had decided that confrontation, not conciliation was the most effective way of working for women's autonomy.

There were many women at the time practising disobedience (perhaps even thousands) as a deliberate political act, and just as Charlotte Despard (a founding member of the Women's Freedom League) refused to acquiesce to male authority and pay her taxes, Rebecca West refused to acquiesce to male authority and pay homage to their intellectual creations. West was aware that it was men who set the social scene and who reserved for themselves the role of *actors*, insisting that women should fit into the supportive place that men had allocated them rather than assert their own aspirations and needs. The writing and the politics of Rebecca West are fused as she refuses to comply with the man-made social pressures, asserts her presence and demands that men react to *her* visibility, not she to theirs. Defying the rules of decorum and deference she joined the other rebellious women at *The Freewoman* (Dora Marsden, Mary Gawthorpe, Grace Jardine and Rona Robinson) and helped to dispel the image of woman as decorative and docile.

The identification of an enemy demands the recognition of his vulnerabilities and along with the staff at *The Freewoman* (and the Suffragettes, Christabel Pankhurst among them), West wasted no time in selecting male sexuality as a target. Such a strategy was doubly advantageous for not only could it help to undermine the plausibility of male arguments in relation to their own nature, it also helped to destroy the credibility of their case in relation to female nature, for according to men it was unthinkable that a proper woman would broach the subject of male sexuality – and venereal disease. So in ringing and resounding tones the topic was taken up by the rebels.[1]

Of *The Freewoman*, Rebecca West later wrote that the 'greatest service that the paper did its country was its un-blushingness', for 'it mentions venereal disease loudly and clearly and repeatedly and in the worst possible taste' and therefore 'by its candour did an immense service to the world by shattering, as nothing else would, as not the mere cries of intention towards independence had ever done, the romantic conception of women' (*Time and Tide*, 1926: quoted in Marcus, 1982, p. 6). It was this disobedience, this failure to comply with the rules of 'woman's true nature' on the part of the staff at *The Freewoman* which 'smashed the romantic pretence that women had as a birth-right the gift of perfect adaptation' to men, and established that women had an identity of their own they were perfectly capable of defining. Those at *The Freewoman* helped lay to rest (at least tempor-arily) the myth that women 'were in a bland state of desire-less contentment which, when they were beautiful reminded the onlooker of a goddess, and when they were plain were more apt to remind them of cabbage' (ibid.).

Many men were in the habit of insisting that women were perfectly content with their lot and would not want independence even if it were handed to them, but if the men were going to be believed then it was necessary that women should agree with them. When a number of women were asserting fiercely and frequently – and heaven forbid, in public – that they were *not* content, that they demanded their independence and were determined to obtain it, then male pronouncements about female fulfilment lost much of their authority.

Rebecca West indicated that she was not at all reluctant to reveal the convenient and self-interested nature of male rationales about woman's disposition for she recognised that if society could be persuaded that women were indeed content with their lot there would be no reason for change. However, it was an entirely different matter when men were forced to admit 'that women were vexed human beings who suffered intensely from male-adaptation to life, and that they were tortured and dangerous if they were not allowed to adapt themselves to life' (ibid.). It was crucial argued West that men should have to give up their practice of seeing women only in relation to themselves and that they should be made to take women into account as an autonomous force outside their control. This, she said, was 'the keystone of the modern Feminist movement' (ibid.): it was a principle apparent in her writing then and one no less applicable today.

I am elated by her words and endorse her advice to the full, yet I remain puzzled in two respects: firstly, I wonder how these rebellious words could have been erased from our cultural heritage to the point where we could have believed that our predecessors were tame and timid souls, setting their sights solely on suffrage (and this is an issue I will return to) and secondly I wonder how this young woman came to hold her uncompromising convictions. Hers was not a philosophy learnt once she joined the staff at *The Freewoman* but one which she had been practising for some time and which propelled her towards *The Freewoman* at the age of eighteen.

She was born Cicily Isabel Fairfield in 1892 and was the third of three daughters. Her father, Charles Fairfield was in the Coldstream Guards but left to take up journalism in the attempt to support his family, a task at which he was relatively unsuccessful, partly because of his predilection for gambling. However, he did help to provide an intellectual climate and Rebecca West has said of her childhood that she had 'grown up in an air thick with conversation about literature, politics, music and painting' (quoted in Marcus, 1982, p. 3). Much of the cultural and all of the musical influence was provided by her mother, Isabella Campbell, whom Rebecca West loved intensely and who, despite the dire financial straits in which she often found herself and her family, struggled to provide her daughters with a sound education as a means of earning their livings. She must have been gratified by the results for the eldest daughter Letitia went on to become a medical practitioner (who argued *for* birth control but *against* the rationale that it was in the interest of a 'better' race to reduce the population of the working class, see *Time and Tide*, 1928, p. 554), while Winifred was an outstanding student at the Maria Grey Training College and went on to achieve considerable distinction as an educator.

While it may not seem remarkable to Rebecca West that she and her sisters were all capable of financial independence – for they were not reared to be parasites, or 'Ladies of Loot' as she was fond of calling them – I find this somewhat surprising, for more than seventy years later it is still not the norm for young women to declare that they are committed to self-support. We have even devised explanations such as the 'fear of success' syndrome (see Matina Horner, 1974) in our attempts to account for women's reluctance to seek economic (and emotional) independence, and certainly the discouragement to aspire to anything other than the appropriate women's jobs was no less then than it is now.

Having spent her early childhood in London, Rebecca West returned to Edinburgh with her family at the age of ten and won a scholarship to the George Watson's Ladies College. She says of this period – with a tinge of bitterness with which I can readily identify – 'I saw in my own education some of the things which eat the power out of women. My fellow pupils and I were not deterred from preparing to earn our livings, because it was evident that for the most part our parents would refuse to support us in idleness; but it was tactfully suggested to us that, rather than attempt to storm the world by genius and personality, we had better court it by conformity to convention and "lady-likeness" ' (*The Clarion*, 14 February 1913).

As she continues to describe her schooling one is struck not by how much things have changed for women during the twentieth century but how much they have remained the same. ' "To take a strong line on anything" was to be regarded as carrying dynamite in one's head to the public danger,' she writes, indicating the way women are channelled into invisibility and non-action. But even during her school days she displayed her capacity for defiance when 'As a child of fourteen I was nagged and worried for wearing a Votes-for-Women badge,' she says. 'Moral passions were discouraged and there was engendered in the girls a habit of compromise and avoiding decisions. Power does not lie that way,' adds West (ibid.).

She excuses little: 'on every essential point where lying was possible, my teachers lied to me,' she says, and 'On the subject of history their mendacity reached its height, and they preached pessimism with a very strange vigour,' as they produced a stainless (and womanless) history of England by a process of elimination. It was 'a lucky chance that snatched the blessing of education from me at the age of fifteen,' she continues, for this 'left me free to study life from the angle of the suffrage movement, which removed any inclination I might have had towards meekness and unqualified admiration of the Government' (ibid.).

West states that had she been less fortunate she might have continued her education and been seduced into being lady-like and resigned, and this theme that formal education is not at all a good thing for women is one which runs through women's writing through the twentieth century with Virginia Woolf insisting in 1938 that education was so damaging to women that their only choice was to remain *outsiders*. Mary Ritter Beard, during the 1930s and 1940s, made the same point when she claimed that the education system had been designed by man and was intended to provide a good account of himself and his past, and it was ludicrous to extend this 'privilege' to woman who, the more time she spent being educated would become more familiar with her own deficiencies in men's eyes. Three outstanding, astute and audacious women who have all argued that men's education of women (for men still control education with 97 per cent of the government of education in England and Wales for example residing in male hands, Eileen Byrne, 1978), is a training in *womanliness*, and is to be avoided. Suggesting that women are discriminated against in men's education is not a new idea but an old one (see Dale Spender, 1982a) as Rebecca West's account testifies.

No doubt many women today could identify with West's position when she came to her understandings of the relationship between the sexes not because of her education but in spite of it. It was *outside* the system that her ideas were forged and she has many regrets for those who are locked *inside* the system: 'A girl who goes to an elementary school is taught the same lies that I was in the same atmosphere of sex-subordination,' she writes, 'And she has no leisure in which to stretch herself and find out what she really is. Not for her are the outdoor exercise and long walks that give one fearlessness. Not for her the unchecked desultory reading which is the proper food for every hungry mind. Even if she does not belong to the class where even the babies have to earn their keep,' she states, focusing on the issue of women's work and pay (or absence of it) to which she would return again and again 'she will be busied by housework' (*The Clarion*, 14 February 1913). This was a fate West considered herself lucky to escape when her initial career choice was the theatre.

In 1908 she returned to London and enrolled at The Royal Academy of Dramatic Art: it was during this period that with characteristic wit and audacity Cicily Fairfield adopted the name Rebecca West 'after playing the strong-willed character of that name in Ibsen's *Rosmersholm*' (*Time and Tide*, 1923, p. 149). At times she also made use of another pseudonym – Rachel East!

Her career on the stage was, however, a brief one.

Reading and writing (and women's emancipation) were for Rebecca West a passion and for years before she joined *The Freewoman* at the age of eighteen she had been almost compulsively practising her craft. She was in her element when she was able to combine her love for reading and writing, her enthusiasm for a better world, and her keen analysis and wit, as she did on this new feminist periodical which was committed to describing and explaining experience as it impinged on women and without regard to the offence it may give men.

One of the clues to her ability to cut through the murk and mire of man-made myths is I think her complete condemnation of the idea that women should be self-sacrificing: she mercilessly mocked 'the idea that women ought to sacrifice the development of their own personalities for the sake of men and children' (*The Clarion*, 13 December 1913), and declared that not only was this a most convenient belief as far as men were concerned, but it was a sin for any human being to cease striving for self-development. In scathing tones West declared that it was absurd that 'a woman should from her childhood be guarded from the disturbance of intellectual effort and should pass through a serenely sentimental adolescence to a home' where 'the tranquil flame of her unspoiled soul should radiate purity and nobility upon an indefinitely extended family' (ibid.). With her damning denunciation of self-sacrifice for women and her avowed intention and discernible habit of practising self-development in preference to self-denial, Rebecca West repeatedly recognised, and repudiated, many of the conventions which encouraged women to support men rather than themselves. She was an excellent example of what a woman *could* do – then and now – if she determined to dispense with approval for her womanliness (or femininity) as defined by men.

She was unequivocal in her declaration that the relationship between the sexes was a problem which would not be resolved by delicate discussions in polite circles or settled by amicable means: for her there was a sex war in progress and she considered herself in a permanent state of battle. While she made sure that wherever possible women who were playing their part in the battle should be seen to be united she felt little need to display a magnanimous attitude to those women who courted the favour of men and who coyly cooed that they were content: the 'Lady of Loot' – and Mrs Humphrey Ward – felt her sting as much as any man. But she endorsed the militancy of the Suffragettes and must have infuriated many with her rational insistence that the Suffragettes' actions were mild in comparison to the betrayal and treachery of the politicians: in 'The Mildness of Militancy: a storm in a tea house' written in response to the burning of a tea house in Kew Gardens, West declares that women's suffrage has been strangled by the fat hands of fools and knaves, that Mrs Pankhurst has shown remarkable clemency, and that being interrupted during a concert or having a golf green destroyed is only a crude way of calling the nation to higher things (*The Clarion*, 28 February 1913).

West was quite open in her praise of Christabel Pankhurst on occasions, for she 'did an infinite service to the world by her articles on venereal disease', although admittedly West rather detracts from this when she adds in the next sentence: 'The content of them was not too intelligent' (Marcus, 1982, p. 5). Despite later political differences with Mrs Pankhurst there is no doubting Rebecca West's admiration for her, and in the essay she wrote on Mrs Pankhurst in 1933 ('A Reed of Steel' in *The Post Victorians*) West portrays her in heroic proportions.

Until I came across Rebecca West's account of Emily Wilding Davison's death and its significance I had only been familiar with versions which represented her as neurotic and which robbed her actions of meaning or magnificence. When Rebecca West gives *her* interpretation of Davison's life and death the distance between men's view of women's protest and the feminist view becomes startlingly clear. Evidently derogatory and dismissive accounts of Davison's actions were not uncommon at the time and Rebecca West recognised the reasons behind such a portrayal and effectively countered the woman-hating of the press, calling it by a feminist name – violence against women. That the patriarchal version of Emily Davison is the one which predominates in any reference where historians have deigned to mention her is but an illustration of the stainless and womanless history of which

West was so critical, and which has been produced by those in power.

Using the force of understatement West writes of Davison that 'she led a very ordinary life for a woman of her type and times. She was imprisoned eight times; she hunger struck seven times; she was forcibly fed forty-nine times. That is the kind of life to which we dedicate our best and kindest and wittiest women' (*The Clarion*, 20 June 1913). Davison's actions, West makes it quite clear, were not the product of a flighty, dramatic, or even deranged mind but were born of deep moral conviction, courage, seriousness of purpose and a determination to do one's duty, for Davison had been 'a woman of learning: she had taken honours in both the English schools at Oxford and classics and mathematics in London University. When she became a militant suffragist she turned her back on opportunities of distinction as a journalist and teacher. More than that,' adds West, who appreciated the precarious nature of the life the suffragettes led, 'she entered a time of financial insecurity; no comfortable background offered her ease between battles' (ibid.).

Battles they were, and horrendous ones at that, and West makes no attempt to spare the reader's finer feelings when she describes the hell that Emily Davison went through at the hands of the government. From the barbarism of forced feeding to the wanton cruelty of turning an icy water hose on Davison in her cell, West lays out the case against the tormentors of women. For the tragedy of Davison's death West places the blame squarely at the feet of the government, the reprehensible and irresponsible male government, and in subdued style states that 'if, when we walked behind her bier on Saturday, we thought of ourselves doing a dead comrade honour, we were wrong. We were making a march of penitance behind a victim we allowed the Government to do to death' (ibid.).

But it is not enough that Emily Davison should have died in the struggle for women's emancipation, West continues. Mrs Pankhurst, out of prison under the infamous Cat and Mouse Act introduced by the tormentors, had tried to attend Davison's funeral and had been arrested: 'Mrs Pankhurst was very ill, so ill that her nurse had tried to dissuade her

from rising for the funeral, lest she should die on the way.
And now she was taken back to Holloway and the hunger
strike. I felt a feeling that is worse than grief' (ibid.).

That there is a war being waged by men against women
is a fact powerfully conveyed by West throughout the article
and she retaliates in a way that would be readily understood
by feminists past and present when she brings together the
government, the press, and Jack-the-Ripper, branding them
all as foe with their practice of violence against women. 'The
mishandling of women has its roots in horror,' she writes, for
'there is an obscene kind of madness that makes men torture
women.' It is a madness demonstrated upon Davison's death
by the press when '*The Manchester Guardian* whimpered evil
of the dead last week; so party passion can turn fools to
knaves. The unspeakable *Pall Mall Gazette*, whose pages in
their technical excellence and spiritual nauseousness remind
one of an efficiently managed sewage farm, had a vulgar
leader with a comic title on the death of Emily Davison'
(ibid.).

These words of West were written seventy years ago:
what has changed? One of the few differences I can detect is
that today we have no public platform like *The Clarion* which
carried feminist views and no feminist journalists who are
permitted to be as outspoken and outrageous as Rebecca
West. I suspect that today these articles of West's which
clearly named men as the enemy would undoubtedly be
called man-hating and probably rejected by most editors if
they were slightly amended to take account of the passing of
time and were submitted under the name of Cicily Fairfield.
My own (limited) experience with journalism has suggested
that the only feminist articles which are acceptable are the
ones which have a 'light touch' which are 'witty and
amusing'. 'None of this whining and complaining', I have
been informed, and I can only muse upon the social values
which would make it seem ludicrous that the working class
should portray classism in a light and witty way, and that
blacks should only write of racism in a humorous tone, while
those same values dictate that it makes good sense that
women should abstain from 'man-hating' in a woman-hating
society.

Like West I believe there is a sex war going on: I can see
that men are devaluing her today in much the same way as
they did earlier this century. 'The anti-feminism was un-
believable,' she has said, but I have no difficulty in believing
it. There is no qualitative difference between the omission
of the Suffragettes' struggle from the history books and
the omission of Rebecca West from the history of English
journalism: there is no qualitative difference between the
devaluation of Emily Wilding Davison in the *Pall Mall
Gazette* and the devaluation of Rebecca West's feminism
in the few biographical accounts of her that men have
written.

Gordon Ray (1974) has written a book on the love affair
of Rebecca West and H. G. Wells. Ray begins with the young
woman who joined the staff of *The Freewoman* in 1911 and
says: 'If she also expounded feminist doctrine with an
assurance amounting to fanaticism, this was after all what
the subscribers to the *Freewoman* expected for their three
pennies; no doubt she had her private reservations', he adds
with what I can only suppose was wishful thinking, for there
is no evidence that Rebecca West *thought* one thing and *wrote*
another: on the contrary she reveals a consistent integrity.
What Gordon Ray thinks of feminism however is readily
suggested by his statement that at *The Freewoman*, her
'articles soon became the most interesting feature of this
otherwise rather shrill and bloodless journal' (p. 8). He
doesn't like West's feminism and he does his best to divest her
of it as quickly as possible: with marked relief and little
evidence he states: 'At the very moment when she showed
herself to be women's answer to Shaw, Chesterton and Wells,
she had lost her faith in the suffragist cause' (p. 27). As
Rebecca West was a feminist then and is a feminist now, one
can only marvel at Ray's imaginative powers. Before he
eliminates West's feminism from his discussion, however, he
throws in a few little gems on the way, one of the best ones
being an explanation for her 'emotional outbursts'; they
were the result of her 'trouble' with Wells. So are women's
political problems reduced to the vagaries of their
(heterosexual) love life. Ray would only have had to read
(closely) some of West's journalism to recognise that it was

precisely this conception of women which Rebecca West derided.

When West left *The Freewoman* and joined *The Clarion* in 1912, all was not going well with Wells, states Ray, and this was exemplified in her writing for 'she was increasingly caught up in the passions of the feminist cause, passions which raged with particular violence at this period because the Women's Suffrage amendment to the Franchise Bill was being defeated' (p. 16). What I found cause for celebration, Ray finds cause for complaint when he says 'Rebecca gradually threw aside all restraints on her writing. Her revulsion reached its climax in a tirade of 18 April 1913, called "The Sex War", most of the paragraphs in which end with the refrain: "Oh, men are miserably poor stuff!" ' (ibid.). Still, it all ends well as far as Ray is concerned: 'As she freed herself from her preoccupation with feminism in *The Clarion*,' he writes, Wells approved of her writing more and more, and the relationship improved!

'What do you see as the fundamental issue?' I asked Rebecca West in March 1982. 'Contempt' she replied, 'the terrible contempt in which men hold women.' (1982b) She felt the force of that contempt when she supported women's suffrage but we feel the force of it in that it has helped to dismiss and deny her contribution and to remove her from our experience and understanding. There *has* always been a women's movement this century, and Rebecca West has always counted herself among its members, but a patriarchal society has taken every care to ensure that we did not know about it and that we were not quickly drawn to her. If there is one thing we should be thankful for it is feminist publishers for in their actions of reclaiming and reprinting Rebecca West we are assured of an alternative to the patriarchal distortions.

When Rebecca West took her stand against men early this century they did not always respond with the suave (insidious?) devaluation as Gordon Ray does in contemporary times, but were more prone to act with rancour and to seek revenge. But this was part of the rationale behind militancy because when men behaved in a violent way towards women it was impossible for them to argue at the same time that they were benevolently disposed towards the fair sex, that they would behave only courteously and chivalrously towards women and extend to them protection, and therefore there was no need for women to advance their own independent interests. If for centuries women had been robbed by men of the means of explaining the world in their own interest as Matilda Joslyn Gage (1893) claims, then this was one period of history when a group of women turned the tables and robbed men of the opportunity to explain the world in a way which suited their own male purposes. This was a period when women seized (some) power, and the exhilaration of the experience shines clearly through Rebecca West's writing.

Men do not implore women to be womanly, to be pure and virtuous, to retire from the public sphere and practise self-sacrifice, marriage and maternity, out of any consideration of women's interests proclaimed Rebecca West throwing down the gauntlet, but because it is in their *own* interest. 'Pure selfishness is the motive of men's desire to oppress women,' she asserts, and 'Antifeminists from Chesterton down to Dr Lionel Tayler [the author of *The Nature of Woman* later fiercely reviewed by West] want women to specialise in virtue. While men are rolling round the world having murderous and otherwise sinful adventures of an enjoyable nature, in commerce, exploration or art, women are to stay at home earning the promotion of the human race to a better world. This,' she adds with a final flourish, 'is illustrated by the middle-class father who never goes to church himself but always sends his wife and daughters' (*The Clarion*, 20 December 1912).

Her taunts invariably found their target and men were predictably provoked – and reacted accordingly, and their at times frenzied and abusive responses helped to demonstrate that there was a sex-war going on!

Being harassed for her outspoken support of women's independence and her castigation of male tyranny was a routine experience for West who began many of her articles with an inventory of the 'objective' male objections of the preceding week. This further act of defiance also helped to intensify the battle. One example of her failure to be intimidated occurred when she wrote an article on the then Home

Secretary, Mr McKenna, entitled 'A Prig in Power' (*The Clarion*, 10 January 1913) in which she held up to scrutiny and called for the condemnation of McKenna's actions over Florence Seymour.

Florence Seymour was pregnant and unmarried and the father of her child was convicted of murder. To avoid the stigma of being an unmarried mother and to protect the interests of the child, Florence Seymour requested permission to marry the father. Mr McKenna refused. 'It matters far more that a woman should have a beautiful and healthy child than that she should have a legitimate child,' wrote Rebecca West, 'but the fact remains that most people do not think like that. They will treat Florence Seymour as an unclean person who has been meddling with important things in an unpleasant manner' (ibid.) and Mr McKenna has no right to refuse permission for marriage. He has exceeded his powers argues West persuasively for he has no right to punish Florence Seymour and no right to inflict additional punishment on the convicted father. It is sufficient to execute the criminal, without preventing him from making peace with his God, and increasing his torture by demanding that he contemplate the fate which awaits Florence Seymour.

Not a highly provocative attack, one would have thought: just a matter of exposing some of the limitations of the powers of reasoning of the Home Secretary. But it was on behalf of the woman that Rebecca West was making her case, and the result was quite heated male criticism of West. 'A spiteful unmarried female churchwoman brought up on the knees of curates' is how West begins her article in *The Clarion* two weeks later giving some idea of the way men define women who appear to get on quite well without them. 'That is how I strike a gentleman living in Petersfield. The high quality of imagination which has enabled him to detect the curates' knees in my article alone differentiates him from many other correspondents who have been angered by my protest against Mr McKenna's prohibition of Florence Seymour's marriage. They are all men,' adds West, making it quite clear that women do not share men's view on this matter – when women should be in a position to speak with more authority than men – for 'No woman has spent her time writing the sentence which in one form or another I have read constantly during this week: "In the eyes of all right-thinking persons there is no stain whatsoever upon Florence Seymour and her illegitimate child" ' (*The Clarion*, 24 January 1913). Women knew better than to believe such nonsense: they knew the penalties a male dominated society could exact from the unmarried mother who challenged the elaborate edifice of male property rights and the psychological injunctions that no woman could be complete without a man.

McKenna was only one of the prominent men to have had his intellectual capacity doubted and derided by West and it is the absence of reverence for male status and the absence of concern for the consequences, which symbolises the *permission* that West represents today. I *know* that females are required to massage male egos, to – in the words of Virginia Woolf – reflect men at twice their natural size – for this is one of the ways that the illusion of male mastery is maintained. It is hard for women to break free from those unwritten but deeply engrained rules which make us refrain from showing up a man in public: instead our training and social pressure prompts us to pretend ignorance of male ineptitude, to gloss over glaring errors, to change topics of conversation so that a man may appear at his best and most impressive. And we smile all the while that we do it. I *suspect* that even the most elementary research project would disclose a veritable 'underworld' of women's meanings – communicated by glance or gesture – as women make unspoken arrangements to 'rescue' a man in difficulty and without fuss or disturbance, restore him to his prestigious place. We perform these services so often and the fact that they are not talked about, not widely recognised as part of women's daily reality, probably has much to do with the understanding that if women were to document and legitimate the enormous amount of unfair unpaid work they are required to do in the task of emotionally managing men, they would in all likelihood stop. They might even start reflecting men at their natural size, as West did, and begin to put an end to the illusion of male superiority.

Rebecca West encouraged women to see and make real

this aspect of oppression. As Jane Marcus has said, Rebecca West attacked the concept of service to men as 'dangerous and reactionary . . . self sacrifice was the most mortal of sins, a sin against life itself.' As Virginia Woolf and Mary Beard were to do later (and as countless women had done before, see Dale Spender, 1982b), she urged women to break free from the belief in their own oppression and the behaviour required by it: she roused them to weed out the victim in their souls. 'A woman must no longer choose the role of the woman behind the great man, mother, sister, lover or wife to his genius. She must stop being the muse and become mistress of her own art, her own science, herself,' states Marcus (1982) summarising West's philosophy (p. 3).

Her politics were put into practice in her writing: she saw men without their aura of superiority, as they are seen by many women and in a way they prefer not to see themselves, and she defiantly broke the taboo and broadcast what she saw. And she did so in celebratory and scintillating style.

I can imagine how the much revered and respected H. G. Wells must have felt when as a literary figure lauded for his ability to portray female sexuality in an audacious way (and before he met Rebecca West) he opened his copy of *The Freewoman* (19 September 1912) to read the review of his latest novel, *Marriage*, written by a nineteen-year-old woman: 'he is the old maid among novelists' was her opinion, 'even the sex obsession that lay clotted on *Ann Veronica* and *The New Machiavelli* like cold white sauce was merely old maid's mania.' West cleverly reverses the value system and berates Wells for his fussy and spinsterish mind – and his inability to perceive women's autonomous sexuality.

Dr Lionel Tayler also finds himself publicly ridiculed and his weakness held up for all the world to see (by a woman! a young woman!! a vivacious and beautiful woman!!!) on the publication of his book *The Nature of Woman*. She defies his whole thesis and mocks his mediocrity, and will not even give him credit for his authority as a biologist (his learning is not impressive, West states and the book 'contains nothing that was not known to all those of us who went to school after the passing of Mr Forster's Education Act of 1870'). And, she declares, his style is abysmal: 'He begins a sentence with a panegyric of conjugal love, and after twenty-four panting lines is in at the death with a discussion of classical education. He does not so much split his infinitives but disembowel them. He encourages a most devastating eruption of footnotes, side headings and appendices.' And for what? To reveal that the behaviour of biologists could be much the same then as it can be now as they try and give scientific weight to self-interested prejudice. *Our* response today, however, is often markedly different from West's and it is worth asking whether we might not be better served by laughing at those who insist that a woman's hormones are the root of all evil or that because gibbons (but not chimpanzees or spiders) behave in a certain way so too should women (see Ruth Hubbard, 1981). Would it be more effective to respond with merriment and mirth rather than seriously try to counter these absurd (but male-convenient) 'truths'?

'Dr Tayler considers womanliness to be a state of holy and sickly imbecility,' writes West. 'Woman is sacred only if she fulfils two conditions. She must be physically so feeble that she cannot play games or take any exercise, and creep along from petty sickness to petty sickness to the malady of motherhood, over the painfulness of which he gloats sentimentally. She must also have lost her reason,' explains West, as 'he insists on the moral necessity of her imbecility because he declares that if she uses her reason she will quarrel with her husband. And anyway "Woman is a bad reasoner at best, but she is a good intuitionist. . . ." ' (*The Clarion*, 7 March 1913). West leaves no doubt that only a very debilitated faculty for reason would ever have to resort to reasoning in this scientific way and it must have been apoplectic-making to some of these prestigious men to have their reputations ridiculed and ruined by this 'uppity' woman.

But some of West's most fiery and fearless efforts (the ones that Gordon Ray called fanatical) were reserved for the political figures, particularly those who were using their power to obstruct women's suffrage and to maltreat and torture women.

Commenting on militancy and Mr Asquith, Rebecca West informed the Prime Minister that he was a lucky man for if it had been Mrs Pankhurst's 'will that Mr Asquith should ascend to Heaven by the aid of dynamite, many women would have been delighted to arrange the dynamite. I should have been very sorry had they done so,' says West with a semblance of seriousness, for 'I dislike the duty imposed on me by the suffrage movement of constantly writing about this least remarkable Yorkshireman who ever lived. But I should dislike still more writing about his corpse. For then I should have to show a decent respect to the dead' (*The Clarion*, 28 February 1913).

Sometimes the sarcasm was more searing: 'There can be no more damning indictment of the nation than the fact that it allows Mr Asquith to decide the question of woman suffrage. Is not the idea of letting Mr Asquith decide anything on earth not enough to blot out the sun in heaven?' asks West, assessing the strengths and weaknesses of the man. 'He would have made an excellent butler,' she adds, taking his measure, and then proceeds with a most provocative account of his potential: 'I can imagine that owlish solemnity quite good and happy polishing the plate or settling a question of etiquette in the servants' hall. Such flunkey minds, afflicted at birth with an irremedial lack of dignity, must invariably be attracted by the elaborate, insincere ceremony of party politics. . . . Mr Asquith, undistinguished in his crimes, expedites by his clumsy thwackings at women from behind the bars of authority' (*The Clarion*, 1 August 1913).

Rebecca West – and thousands of other women – held Asquith in contempt, not out of any preconceived notion or prejudice, but because of the bigotry of the man and his bullying and betrayal of women in relation to suffrage. One assumes that H. G. Wells (with whom Rebecca West was becoming increasingly involved) was not sympathetic to such attacks on Asquith: in 1911 he had written an article for *The Freewoman* entitled 'Mr Asquith Will Die' (7 December) in an attempt to dissuade the Suffragettes from directing their energy towards Asquith. Evidently his opinion on this matter carried little weight with Rebecca West who continued to deplore and deride the Prime Minister's ineptitude, intolerance and irresponsibility.

H. G. Wells does, however, serve to raise the issue of the difficulties which are at times embodied in the shape of male champions of women's rights. This is an issue no less present or problematic today than it was at the beginning of this century (and before) for while there have been men who have publicly declared their support for women's liberation (and their declarations, predictably have often been treated as more authoritative than those of women), in their failure to appreciate that the personal is political their behaviour has often given many feminists cause for concern.

This may constitute a dilemma for women, for to publicly attack Bertrand Russell for example, for his attitude towards women (particularly to his wives) could be construed as nothing short of 'embitterment' on the part of the non-discriminating 'battle-axes', when the good man was championing women's cause and lending it so much prestige and authority (Russell was the first parliamentary candidate to stand on a women's suffrage platform, see Dale Spender, 1982b, p. 475). The result has often been that prominent and 'radical' men have enjoyed a measure of *immunity* as women have held their peace. Elizabeth Robins, however, made no such exceptions: she openly criticised the contributions of George Bernard Shaw and H. G. Wells and called them opportunism (see Marcus, 1980, p. 9) and Rebecca West made no such exception for David Lloyd George, who because he was supposedly not against women's suffrage was sometimes seen as a man to be courted, not one to be condemned.

With accuracy and acerbity, Rebecca West shows up Lloyd George, catching him in an act of magnanimity – and malice! Having been awarded £1,000 in a libel suit, Lloyd George donated the money to build a village institute in Llanystumdwy. He opened the institute – in the presence of the press – in what West describes as a 'debauch of vulgarity' (*The Clarion*, 27 September 1912). The press, however, were not the only ones present as witnesses of Lloyd George's generosity: 'Some suffragettes turned up at the opening ceremony. They reminded Mr Lloyd George that the question of the enfranchisement of women had not been settled. They were tactful. They did not point out the plain truth – that it is galling for women to be cheated out of their citizenship by such an inefficient person as Lloyd George,' states West, paving the way for her blistering denunciation which was to follow.

The women's reminder to Lloyd George was reasonable: for decades they had been struggling for suffrage and they had been repeatedly deceived and duped by dishonourable politicians. But, as on so many previous occasions, these women who were giving voice to their genuine grievance were dealt with in the most abhorrent manner. They were brutally treated.

'Think of a mob of screaming, shrieking men, convulsed with liberalism, throwing themselves on singlehanded women, beating them with sticks and stones, tearing out their hair in handfuls, and stripping them down to the waist!'. West writes in terrible anger, 'Think of them dragging the bleeding bodies of their captives towards the village pump, pitching them over hedges, and trying unsuc-cessfully to dip them in the river' (ibid.). This is the 'un-governable frenzy' of the 'objective' sex, described by Matilda Joslyn Gage in 1893, although called by men by another name.

One might ask what the Right Honourable Mr Lloyd George, the champion of liberty, was doing while his audience at the village institute engaged in these barbaric practices? *He* was calling *them* by another name as well in his speech:

> There is no country where political warfare is fought under
> stricter and more honourable rules of fair play and
> personal chivalry than in Great Britain. That is a worthy
> pride and boast for this land and they fight all the more
> effectively because they fight honourably (quoted by West,
> *The Clarion*, 27 September 1912).

At the time of this particular pronouncement on honour, states West, Lloyd George was observing a Suffragette being pinioned and punched by one of the worthy fellows whom he was holding up to the world as an example of the fair play, decency, honesty and chivalry of the British political system. In a tone meant to convey regret, Lloyd George con-tinued his observations on the fate of the suffragettes: 'I would do my best to protect their lives, but I cannot be

responsible any longer' (ibid.). Ragingly West retorts: 'it was
only by a miracle that his fellow countrymen did not take the
hint.'

That women are perceived as not fully human, as lacking
the human needs and aspirations that are accorded to men is
a point that has been made by women for as long as men have
held power (see Dale Spender, 1982b). It was a point that
Rebecca West was making in this indictment of Lloyd George
who could insist on the honour, integrity and chivalry of men
even while they were brutally mishandling women who were
doing nothing more nor less than expressing *their* wish to join
the political circles of which Lloyd George had spoken so
highly.

This double standard of one rule for women and another
for men is as widespread now as it was then. Men were not
induced to outrage by political struggles *per se*: these were to
be lauded and applauded as Lloyd George had indicated –
when they were conducted by men! The case of the Irish
protests revealed that men did not necessarily respond
brutally or repressively to militancy but could rather display
serious consternation and concern – when it was men who
were being militant over a male issue! What incensed men
was that women should seek to usurp the male prerogatives
of power and action and to become a force in their own
interest. And what incensed Rebecca West was the irrationality, cruelty and hypocrisy of these so called champions of
liberty.

In contemporary times there are few if any equivalents
to Rebecca West's protest which appeared in *The Clarion*.
While not a paper of the establishment it nonetheless represented a significant lobby and could be quite influential: it
was read by many men as well as women. Today, men, and
policemen, may still treat women brutally (as happens on
occasions when women demonstrate) and politicians may
still look on and express their regret – and powerlessness!
But the following day there is unlikely to be a broadside
against the men involved in any of the major socialist or left
publications. The 'incident' may be reported but the blistering denunciation of the type that Rebecca West delivered is
unlikely to be carried in a paper which perceives men as the

mainstay of its readership. So much for women's progress in the twentieth century.

At the time, Lloyd George's abominable behaviour *was* reported in the establishment press – although such reports did not share many of the features of West's writing. But West was quick to point out that the exposure of Lloyd George was not because there had been a shift in values and that there was now sympathy for the women's cause. There are many dimensions of power, she warned her readers and if we are now witnessing critical reports of Lloyd George it is because of some squabble going on among the men themselves. 'Things like this have often happened before,' she says in relation to the violence against women, for 'It has long been the custom of stewards at Cabinet Ministers' meetings to commit vindictive and often indecent assaults on suffragette interrupters. There have been attacks on the lives of many suffragettes,' but such incidents have not found their way to our breakfast tables. At the moment, she continues, 'The Tory papers want to discredit Lloyd George, and to this end they use the pain women have suffered for their principles,' and they use it 'coolly and calculatingly' for 'They have their own axe to grind' (ibid.).

There was no point in women putting their faith in men, argued West, not even socialist men, because there was a conflict of interest between women and men, and men would simply 'protect their own' in the face of any threats from women. The unapologetic declaration of war, the unabashed insistence on it as a necessary and just war is a characteristic which marked Rebecca West then and now. The withdrawal of male approval – a weapon used effectively against women for a long time – appears to have made no impression on West who continued to mock male values and to expose the false nature of male 'protection'. That she did this so openly, unashamedly, and in the spirit of moral responsibility may have enraged many men but inspired many women.

Every aspect of man, and man-governed systems, was grist to her mill and week after week she wrote her stinging and sparkling articles: 'Every man likes to think of himself as a kind of Whiteley's – a universal provider,' wrote Rebecca West in 1912 in the *Manchester Daily Despatch* (26

November). 'The patriarchal system is the ideal for which he longs. He likes to dream of himself sitting on the verandah after dinner, with his wife beside him and the children in the garden, while his unmarried sisters play duets in the drawing room and his maiden aunts hand around the coffee. This maintenance of helpless, penniless, subservient womanhood is the nearest he can get in England to the spiritual delights of the harem.'

In the interest of making this dream come true she explains, man has thought of a multitude of reasons for paying woman less – even when she does the same work – for how else is she to be enticed into giving up her own life in order to serve a man, if not by financial necessity? But because many women want to lead their own lives, and because they can see that no pay and low pay makes marriage compulsory, they have started demanding better pay and the option of earning their living in occupations other than marriage. This is a perfectly reasonable and just demand, states West, but one to which men are likely to react with irrationality and rage – thereby unwittingly revealing the extent of the esteem in which they hold women and the unmasked nature of male chivalry and protection! When 'womanhood declares,' says West, 'that she is no longer helpless, dislikes being penniless, and refuses to be subservient, the men become indignant and inarticulate,' and find themselves caught in a contradictory position.

They have two areas they wish to protect – in their own self-interest – the home and the workplace, and when 'only by the fear of starvation are women coerced into having husbands,' then starving women into marriage means among other things, paying them low wages. Unfortunately, however, men also want to maintain their monopoly on employment and they have to confront the unpalatable fact that lower paid women are often more attractive to employers than higher paid men, with the result that ensuring wives may necessitate the risk of losing jobs. Hence their irrational, inarticulate protest, states West, for men want both wives *and* jobs.

Equal pay for equal work was just a matter of plain common sense to Rebecca West: women's needs are no less than men's, and women's freedom to *choose* paid work or marriage – or *both*, as men had been doing for many a year – was no less precious. And if men were only sensible about this she argued, they might begin to see that they had something to gain as well, for once the compulsory element was removed from marriage, once women were permitted the same job opportunities as men, women would be more likely to choose a companion than accept an employer; 'if there is to be any romance in marriage,' she wrote, 'woman must be given every chance to earn a decent living at other occupations. Otherwise no man can be sure that he is loved for himself alone, and that his wife did not come to the Registry Office because she had no luck at the Labour Exchange' (ibid.).

The male capacity for logic, however, appears to be severely limited for neither then nor now have men shown themselves to be convinced by the reasonableness of the case, and they give every sign of ending the century in the way that they began it – by paying woman less. Despite the passing of legislation such as Equal Pay Acts most sources (including the United Nations' statistics on the position of women) indicate that the gap between women's pay and men's pay is growing greater every year. Men still control the world's resources (more then 99 per cent of them according to United Nations' statistics) and therefore can still exercise control over women: seventy years has seen no significant change in the distribution of wealth between the sexes.

Low pay and no pay are the rewards for women's work, says West. Burdened with more than their share of domestic duties women are robbed of leisure (the current UN statistics are that women perform more than two-thirds of the world's work for less than one-tenth of the world's pay), and are victims of a pernicious superstition that women have no need of joy in life. Leisure is considered the just due of men and from childhood through adolescence to adulthood, provision is made for recreational facilities and interesting games, on the assumption that men deserve joy after the hard grind of work (see *The Clarion*, 14 February 1914). This was a fallacious assumption but not one which has been modified with the passing of time: one glance for example at the well-equipped squash and cricket facilities in institutions of higher education, and the impoverished if not absent child-care facilities, indicates that the assumption prevails. Men are still entitled to their leisure while women do the work and while women are seen to have no need of joy. (Having been overwhelmed by men's leisure activities on the television screen I once suggested to a BBC producer that perhaps he might like to do some programmes on women's leisure habits: after thinking about this for a few minutes he asked in a perplexed manner, 'What exactly would they be?'.)

With clarity and precision Rebecca West cut through patriarchal conventions and exposed the male-interest which was their foundation. Her feminist framework – just as relevant today – could take account of virtually all aspects of existence in a man-made society and was well thought out, clear and coherent. It allowed her to identify, immediately, the penalties for women when men suggested a whole range of provisions which were ostensibly for woman's own good. An example of this is the arrangement of domestic science education for women which, no matter how well men dressed it up, suggested to West that this was just another means whereby men could persuade women that service to men was their role in life. She was scathing in her attack, declaring that the introduction of domestic science was just another ploy for cheating girls of an education (*The Freewoman*, 13 November 1911); assuming that poverty is the product of ignorance – and women's ignorance at that – is absurd argued West, and even men should be able to come up with a better analysis and solution than the one which claims that by teaching domestic economy to women, poverty will be eliminated (*The Freewoman*, 6 June 1912). Not even King's College could hope for that particular success, she expostulated.

So many things men have proposed that women do 'for their own good' are not in women's interest at all, argues Rebecca West: it is men, not women who stand to profit from these proposals and the justifications which men provide are nothing other than elaborate trappings designed to conceal the fact that men want women to serve them – in a variety of ways – and are prepared to try and convince rather than coerce women to comply. This is not surprising. Patriarchy is supported by an ideology designed to make the system 'palatable' for women. As with all 'totalitarian' regimes, those in power control the sources of information and promote propaganda which is meant to persuade those without power that it is the most reasonable and desirable form of government. Women are informed that it is to their advantage to support the system.

Feminism has always been concerned with eliminating these ideological niceties and with exposing the crude power basis that the propaganda is meant to camouflage: when it comes to cutting through the cant and uncovering the male self-interest it is intended to conceal, there have been few more effective feminists than Rebecca West. She has turned her wit and her pen against male power and its ideology (and against the women who have been taken in by it.

For *their* own good, says Rebecca West, men have held up to women an ideal of femininity or womanliness which women are obliged to aspire to. Women are assured that it is for their benefit that they should attempt to achieve this elevated state. But while there are many pretty rational-isations about the desirable woman, in essence a feminine or womanly woman is simply one who supports men and a 'man-governed system', and who will go to any lengths to prove her allegiance.

The word 'womanly' makes me alarmed, wrote Rebecca West in 1913 for 'It recalls a painful incident that occurred to my sister and me some years ago in a public park in Harrogate. We were selling *Votes for Women*,' she explains, 'and we offered one to a dear old lady in rustling black silk and a widow's bonnet. With superb vigour she raised her umbrella and brought it down on my sister's head, remark-ing: "Thank God I am a womanly woman!" And since then,' adds West, 'I have noticed that womanliness is a virtue claimed only with aggressive intent' (*The Clarion*, 7 March 1913).

It seems that a feminine woman may be virulent or vitriolic – qualities not usually assumed to be associated with the revered image of womanhood – as long as these qualities are used against other women and in defence of the man-governed system and its decrees. In contrast, women who use their energy to support other women and to question or defy the male-system, are consistently condemned no matter how cautious, courteous or clear headed their criticism. These are the unfeminine women, the feminists! 'I myself have never been able to find out precisely what feminism is,' declared West, 'I only know that people call me a feminist whenever I express sentiments that differentiate me from a doormat' (*The Clarion*, 14 November 1913). Feminists are those dreadful 'uppity' women with opinions of their own, who do not subscribe to men's propaganda about themselves or women, and whose existence therefore – whether meek or mutinous – makes them a target for attack and derision.

Rebecca West has had more than her fair share of devaluation. At least while her writing was confined almost exclusively to journalism, however, she had a platform from which to defend herself and one from which she could embark on attacks of her own, but it was a different matter when she moved into the world of letters and literature as she did in 1916 (with a critical study of Henry James) and in 1918 with her second book, a novel, *The Return of the Soldier* (a select bibliography of Rebecca West's work is included at the end of this chapter). Both books reflect her feminist values and met with a response only too familiar to feminist writers today. The realm of letters was then as it is now controlled by men who did not willingly open their doors to welcome the new writer, the new woman writer who was not won to their cause.

'You cannot imagine the anti-feminism of men like Arnold Bennett,' she said when we spoke (1982b): but I can, for one does not have to look far for his contemporary equivalents. Throughout the twentieth century, and for centuries before, the 'men of letters' have closed ranks and protected their territory from female encroachment.[2] Their techniques have been simple, but effective. Sometimes women writers are pointedly ignored, frequently they are ridiculed and more often than not they are misrepresented, and almost always they are 'minimised'. This treatment of women's contribution helps to ensure that women writers are not centrally significant and not worthy of serious study.

Thus the world of letters remains a male domain. Male

authors predominate in the curriculum: 95 per cent in one women's college in America states Elaine Showalter (1978; p. 318), and 95 per cent in a number of A Level syllabi in England states Anna Walters (1977).[3] Male writers command a disproportionate space in publishing houses: women have never been more than 20 per cent of the published writers states Lynne Spender (1983). Books by men take pride of place in libraries now as they did when Virginia Woolf gazed upon them in 1928 (with even the British Library storing most of the women as 'minor' writers in their depots), and books by men take prominence when it comes to reviews.[4] And few are the places where women writers can make public their grievance and hold men accountable for their protective and restrictive trade practices.

Rebecca West has been on the receiving end of all these forms of discrimination. She has been ignored, she has been wilfully misrepresented at times – particularly as some reviewers have scored their 'clever' points – and today, critical studies of her work consistently devalue her. Despite seventy years of sustained and splendid work, little has changed: Rebecca West can be treated much the same currently as she was treated by Arnold Bernett earlier this century. 'Critics and reviewers tell the most extraordinary lies about me,' she says (1982b): they need to: how else can she be classified as a 'minor' writer?

'It's just poisonous nonsense of one kind or another,' she says, but it is the poisonous nonsense that has been handed out to women writers for generation after generation and which is nothing other than the man-made propaganda designed to convince the community that women are marginal, that their marginality is justified, and that 'man-made' is the mark of quality (1982b).

Citing a representative example, West tells of the professor with an enviable imaginative capacity, who deduced that one of her novels was autobiographical, that it contained *true* accounts of her life and *proved* that her mother was an unsatisfactory character, the implication being, of course, that this explained all West's 'problems'. 'Such incidents just never happened,' says West, almost incredulous that one should find it necessary to explain the form of fiction to a professor of literature (1982b).

Now, as always, however, Rebecca West does not take these insults lying down and apart from a formidable record of threats to sue those who misrepresent her, who 'concoct a tissue of lies' about her, she has also offered to be of assistance to her scholarly critics and on more than one occasion has edited their manuscripts in the interest of accuracy. Needless to say, they have not expressed their gratitude.

Samuel Hynes is one who has devalued her contribution. In 1977, when after years of neglect a selection of Rebecca West's writing was reprinted, Hynes wrote the Introduction, which, says West, fits with neither her life nor her beliefs. As he manages to suggest in this short piece that feminism was a phase in West's life and a phase in which her work was of little significance, I was reassured by Rebecca West's words that Hynes was – to put it charitably – mistaken. No doubt the feminist publishers who have reissued the work which Hynes found so slight, will be equally reassured.

Two of West's novels are omitted from the 1977 collection and Hynes explains their absence: 'In the 1920s there were two novels, both now forgotten,' he states; one was *The Judge* (1922) 'a long melodramatic story of sex, guilt and power, interesting for the autobiographical beginning in Edinburgh, and for the remarks about the nature of man-woman relations, but imaginatively lifeless' (p. xii). The other was *Harriet Hume* (1929), an equally and avowedly feminist novel.

Like Gordon Ray who was convinced that Rebecca West had a 'feminist phase' in her journalistic career, and who almost indecently tried to hurry her out of it and on to 'better' things, Samuel Hynes acknowledges the feminist nature of these two novels, but attempts to put them in 'perspective'. These were not 'the right form for Dame Rebecca's mind to expand in,' he declares loftily, 'and these are her two least successful novels.' We will all be relieved to know that in 'the following decade or so, one can see Dame Rebecca reaching out towards larger subjects' (p. xii) for 'a woman must stretch beyond woman's matters' (p. xviii) if she is to be a worthy writer. Arnold Bennett has his contemporary disciples.

West's first book, *Henry James* 'shows the feminist spirit of the time very clearly,' states Hynes, implying that such an attitude is now passé, and with the condescension of a man evaluating a woman's work adds it 'is at its best when it deals with James' female characters' (p. x). Her second book, *The Return of the Soldier* (1918) 'is a rare kind of book, a woman's war novel' and, as is typical of women in general and the womanly West in particular, shows war 'refracted in the crystal of a woman's enclosed private life'. (Freud has his contemporary disciples, too.) *The Return of the Soldier*, states Hynes, 'is more nearly a "woman's novel" . . . than anything else Dame Rebecca wrote, and one can understand why she chose not to continue in this manner, after such a bright beginning. For it comes too close to being *merely* a woman's novel' (p. xi). It is quite clear that Hynes assumes that the real issues of the world are those which concern men, and if West wants to be a real writer, she had better start taking them on.

Of course, if a woman wants to set her sights on such an ambition she must recognise that it is 'one that must lead a woman away from her private world, to politics and art and history, to law, religion and crime' (p. xi). No wonder West says that he knows little or nothing of her beliefs or her life. What does he think she has been doing all this time? Surely he is not asking us to believe that this woman who was a political journalist, who was supporting herself and her child, who was 'out there on the barricades' as Jane Marcus (1980) has said, was leading an enclosed, protected and private life, as is the way with the fair sex? Surely he is not suggesting that being a woman is a handicap which ensures that women are but minor artists?

Surely he is!

There is one book which redeems West as far as Hynes is concerned: it is *Black Lamb and Grey Falcon* (1937): 'in this one book she cast aside entirely the restrictions of "woman writer" and revealed the true range of her mind' (p. xv). I have not read anything else that Samuel Hynes has written – and have no inclination to do so – but I wonder if he has contemplated the statement that 'in this one book *he* cast aside entirely the restrictions of "man-writer" and revealed the true range of *his* mind.' It is an idea that he could perhaps profitably give some thought to!

Unfortunately, however, Hynes is part of the great propaganda machine and instead of being ridiculed his polemics are more likely to be respected. Young readers coming to the 1977 collection of Rebecca West's work are already being channelled by the selection of information and it would be understandable if they were to base their opinions on what was included in the collection, rather than on what was left out. It would be equally understandable if they were to accept the 'expert's' evaluation of West and to believe that Hynes's interpretation was impartial, in true scholarly tradition; then they could become members of a community which agreed that West's sex – and her feminism – were a disqualification, that *The Judge* and *Harriet Hume* are without substance and interesting only as curios or for their quaint commentary on the man-woman relationship. It is understandable that young readers could take Hynes at his word that these are novels not worth seeking out. And so the system works; another woman is censored and a record of 'great literature' that meets with male approval becomes the cultural heritage.

Reviewing the anthology of Rebecca West's early journalism (West, 1982), Julian Symons (*The Sunday Times*, 1982) follows in the path of Samuel Hynes and states that the work reveals some of the limits of her talent; 'Her style, energetic, lucid and forceful, was and has remained that of an attacking journalist, rather than of a subtle and profound thinker,' and we are left with the impression that while Rebecca West may have been entertaining she was not of sufficient creative or intellectual calibre to warrant entry to the world of letters where the writers of the genuine literary masterpieces (the subtle and profound thinkers and *not* the attacking journalists) have their place.

'The "anarchist feminism" of her youth . . . had much more feminism than anarchism about it,' adds Symons, 'and her interest in political theory was always slight.' While men control the meanings of society then their definition of politics seems ever destined to relate to issues only among themselves and to exclude the question of male power as a political issue.

There are some points for praise in Symons's review but the overwhelming tone is one in which Rebecca West is being put down; conscious of the negative tone that pervades the reviewer states that: 'This is not however the note to end on in writing of an extremely enjoyable book,' but then with a wanton lack of logic concludes that: 'These essays and reviews make up a splendid firework display, but at the end we find with surprise that the coloured lights don't spell out "Revolution" or even "Feminism" but simply "Common Sense".' We are witnessing here the construction of another 'minor' writer, another woman writer who may be of interest to future scholars, who may even be amusing but one who does not deserve a place in the mainstream of our literary culture or whose contribution should be made known to future generations as part of their heritage.

Fortunately, however, Rebecca West has lived long enough to observe this process, which takes time as the events of one generation are edited for consumption by the next: fortunately she is able to correct the record and to expose the distortions men of letters have fashioned in their own favour. It is because she has seen the way women and their work can be negated that she is full of praise for feminist publishers who played no small role in rescuing some of her work from the fate of invisibility. It is feminist publishers who have defied the propaganda; they have reprinted the books that supposedly won't sell and for which they have been informed by authorities that there is no market, they have boldly reissued the 'imaginatively life-less,' the 'unsubtle' and 'unprofound' and otherwise 'best forgotten' books of women writers, they have appreciated the politics men have not noticed, they have acclaimed the women's novels that men have disdained, and valued the 'women's matters' that men have dismissed.

But . . . a few feminist publishers do not a revolution make. It is not just that we have had feminist publishers before who have for a relatively short space of time provided alternative meanings, it is that publication of its own is not sufficient. Rebecca West has been published throughout her lifetime (at least twenty books on my count, not to mention other publications), but this does not assure her of a place in our heritage. West has experienced a lifetime of frustration finding out that her books are unavailable in bookshops, that they cannot be ordered, that they are not reviewed or are pejoratively reviewed, and that in critical circles they are 'without merit'. One book, which *she* considers the best she has ever written ('If ever I've written a good book, that was it'), was treated in the main as a non-event and when 'noticed' it was in a way that she could well have done without! Should Rebecca West sit down with a group of younger women writers today and exchange notes it would soon emerge that when it comes to women's words things haven't changed much during the twentieth century.

West knows that there are just as many male critics today who are as keen to discredit women writers as they were fifty or sixty years ago. She sees them engaged in a masculinist defence, raising their voices in a chorus of plaintive protests to protect their domain: 'Alas! a woman that attempts the pen,' wrote Anne Finch (1661–1720), 'Such an intruder on the rights of men' (1973). Men have defended their rights to the written word, for centuries: it is the way they produce such good opinions of themselves and their work.

But Rebecca West insists that there are women who have been only too willing to help them. If Arnold Bennett has his contemporary equivalents so too does Mrs Humphrey Ward and Rebecca West shows no more sympathy now than she did sixty and seventy years ago for 'women who dance to the pan pipes of the male' (1982b). She finds it very odd that some women should persist with this behaviour. She appreciates that it may be a way of getting jobs – and that women need jobs – but she sees it as a short-term solution and a counter-productive one, and wonders why women have not learnt that it simply perpetuates their dependence on men, not just economically, but psychologically as well. And as might be expected from a woman who so early and so readily dispensed with male approval, Rebecca West has no patience with women who seek it. She finds such behaviour reprehensible and is not averse to calling it wicked and shameless.

She is resigned to the fact that women have not progressed very far this century: 'they are still male property,' she says. She knows that women's word carries neither the same weight nor credibility as men's and we talked of rape, of sexual harassment, of sexual interference with girls and the reluctance of male authorities (from Freud to a local police sergeant) to believe women when it comes to sexual abuse and violence by men. We talked about women being discredited in ways that men are not, about being dismissed because they are 'hard' and 'aggressive' and yet no less dismissed for being pretty and pliant. She spoke of incidents in which women's reputations in the public realm had been ruined by the simple and unsubstantiated assertion that they didn't like children. 'It was a charge you couldn't answer,' she said. 'And a convenient way of preventing women from being selected as parliamentary candidates' (1982b).

For her whole life she has been aware of the operation of the double standard and sees no evidence of its demise: 'You only have to look at the "Obituaries" in *The Times*,' she says with her characteristic verve, 'and you'll find that most of the space is given to men. When women have similar public or personal records they don't even rate a mention' (1982b).

Never has she lost sight of that alternative view which embodies women's values and which enables her to see through the dissembling of men. She has never lost her ability to puncture their pomposity or to attack their self-admiration. So, in her scheme of values Norman Mailer and Sigmund Freud share a similar pathetic fate. She has not been swayed by male authority and has not swerved from her belief that women are autonomous beings with a creative and intellectual energy of their own – which can be used for women's self-interest.

She has intentionally tried to create a space in which women can pursue their own interests, in their own way, and free from the interference of men. Always she has insisted that women should *stop* trying to adapt themselves to men's needs and *start* instead to define and develop their own: always she has preached and practised the belief that there is no future for women in seeking male approval and in moulding themselves in the man-made image of the ideal woman: always she has urged resistance and rebellion – not from a sense of desperation but from a commitment to women's dignity and strength.

She is the evidence of that dignity and strength. She is also the evidence that feminism can be joyous and celebratory, subversive and enriching, daring and dangerous.

Consistently defining the relationship between the sexes as one of war, she nonetheless pays little heed to male opinion. (One of her recent interviewers, Leslie Garis, 1982, appears to have been rather disconcerted by West's scornful 'Oh men', which she used to sum up a whole range of male antics.) West has shown few signs of agreeing with men's assessment of their own importance and overall has treated patriarchal pronouncements more as a source of irritation than serious threat. This is not to suggest that she minimises the resources men have at their disposal and the uses to which they can put them, but she absolutely refuses to be intimidated by their show of power. 'The fundamental folly of Freudianism' is how she witheringly describes one particular power ploy. 'All that nonsense about suffering from penis envy,' she scoffs, and exposes the absurdity of the belief that the unconscious informs little girls that their sex organs are inadequate while those of little boys – which they may never have even seen – are objects to be desired (see Scott, 1972). She is quite adamant that anyone who could believe such a theory would have to be desperate – and would have to feel deeply that women were inferior (West, 1982b). It is the *belief* in such theories that is so damaging for women, says West, who remains a determined heretic.

Rebecca West has witnessed the rise and fall of many movements during the twentieth century but for her there has always been a women's movement. Whether or not it has been in fashion is another matter. But there can be no doubt that whatever other changes have been wrought by the passing of time there have been two constants in Rebecca West's life – her feminism and her writing.

Whether her relationship was with H. G. Wells, her son, or Henry Maxwell Andrews (whom she married in 1930 and who died in 1968), whether she has been in England or one of the many other countries she has visited, whether she was writing fiction, philosophy, biography, criticism, or

journalism, her women's politics – in her living and writing –
remain clear and consistent. She has created for us a rich
resource, which in Jane Marcus's words mark her as 'this
century's great feminist literary critic, philosopher, novelist,
historian and journalist' (1980b, p. 5). Yet it is a resource
which we have been sadly in danger of neglecting. Even now
the critical work and commentary which exists on Rebecca
West is not only sparse but dominated by men[5] and with
predictable results. While Rebecca West has put so much
energy into constructing women's meanings we have put
very little into preserving them and have even run the risk of
permitting her feminist analysis to pass from us. Are we
going to let her be erased and leave it to future generations of
women to reclaim her? For there is no body of feminist knowledge on or about Rebecca West which can be used to refute
and repudiate the patriarchal image which is currently being
constructed. We are in the process of watching one of the most
illuminating feminists of the twentieth century being edited
from the record in the way that countless women from past
centuries have been erased: we have been rightly angered
that this should have occurred in the past but we appear to be
somewhat indifferent about preventing it in the present.

We have to ask what part we are playing in this process
of women's removal from our cultural heritage. When the
women's liberation movement was revitalised in the 1960s,
why is it that we did not flock to Rebecca West's front door and
seek her counsel? How did it happen that some of us could
come to think not just that we were the inventors of women's
protest, but that the women who had for decades been fighting for women were unworthy of attention and unsuitable for
advice? How could we have been taken in by all that propaganda, believed all those lies, when Rebecca West herself had
for so long and so laudably worked to dispel those very
deceptions?

It is ironic that if we begin to ask what we should do then
one of the most profitable sources to which we might turn for
strategies and solutions is the work of Rebecca West. Today
she shows the same spirit as she has done throughout her life,
the same defiance as she did seventy years ago when she
mocked men and their high priests. She is unequivocal in her

contention that the sex-war is just as necessary now as it has been in the past. We need her words: we cannot afford to be accomplices in the act of erasing her from our traditions.

Select bibliography

Fiction

The Return of the Soldier, 1918, The Century Co., New York; Nisbet, London.

The Judge, 1922, Hutchinson, London; Doran, New York; 1980, Virago, London.

Harriet Hume, 1929, Hutchinson London; Doubleday, Doran, New York; 1980, Virago, London.

War Nurse, 1930, Cosmopolitan Book Corp.

The Harsh Voice; Four Short Novels, 1935, Jonathan Cape, London; Doubleday, Doran, New York; 1982, Virago, London.

The Thinking Reed, 1936, The Viking Press, New York; Hutchinson, London, reissued, 1966, Macmillan, London; 1979, Pan, London.

The Birds Fall Down, 1966, Macmillan, London; The Viking Press, New York.

The Fountain Overflows, 1957, Macmillan, London; 1979, Pan, London.

Non-Fiction

Henry James, 1916, Nisbet, London; Henry Holt, New York.

The Strange Necessity: Essays and Reviews, 1928, Jonathan Cape, London; Doubleday, Doran, New York.

Ending in Earnest; a Literary Log, 1931, Doubleday, Doran, New York.

St Augustine (A Biography), 1933, Peter Davies, London; Appleton, New York.

Black Lamb and Grey Falcon: A Journey Through Yugoslavia, 1941, The Viking Press, New York; 1942, Macmillan, London.

The Meaning of Treason, 1947, The Viking Press, New York; 1949, Macmillan, London.

The New Meaning of Treason, 1964, The Viking Press, New York; 1965, Macmillan, London; 1982, Virago, London.

A Train of Powder, 1955, The Viking Press, New York; Macmillan, London.

The Court and the Castle, 1957, Yale University Press, New Haven; 1958, Macmillan, London.

Chapter 3

DORA RUSSELL
Born 1894

A narrow winding road leads to an old white house – with blue trim – perched up high in peaceful surroundings. The entry is through the kitchen and with the exception of the more modern gas cooker looks very much as though it has been carefully maintained but little changed since the house was built. For over sixty years it has been Dora Russell's home and she and her surroundings have grown together. Despite the many upheavals there have been in her life, the many sorrows and joys, there is in the kitchen an atmosphere of warmth and security: this is where food has been prepared and eaten, where there has been animated discussion, where children have been cared for, where life goes on. Opposite the entrance is a huge old dresser with a colourful collection of assorted dishes and ornaments. They have pride of place: they were given to Dora Russell by the women of many different countries in 1958 when she took her Women's Caravan of Peace through most of Europe and helped to show that women were able to communicate across national boundaries and were prepared to work for international understanding and peace.

The Caravan of Peace – like many other activities she has been involved in – may not find its way into the history books where the emphasis is on the collapse of peace not the maintenance of it, nor is it generally described as *political*. But all this does is provide Dora Russell with more evidence to support her position that the world we know has been decreed by men who declare their own behaviour and values as real and important and who will not see or will not understand that there is a vast area of women's politics and women's history – which they ignore at great risk.

No matter how men may describe it Dora Russell has led a richly political life which reflects many of women's priorities: she was one of the early campaigners for birth control information, she has always been concerned with providing fit conditions for children to thrive in and for sixteen years ran one of the most responsible, child-oriented and humanitarian schools. She has been concerned with the creativity of human beings and with working for a society in which human creativity can be fostered. All her adult life she has devoted her energy to preserving peace and the planet, being one of the first in modern times to appreciate the inter-related nature of existence: she was a founding member of the conservation movement and a formulator of what we take for granted today as an ecological view of the world.

And she was – and is – a philosopher, a thinker and explainer of why we are here, and what it all is for. That peace and conservation, co-operation and education, that the encouragement of creative and intellectual life and the care of children are *not* the social priorities of our way of life is to her a fundamental problem and one that she has tried to solve for almost seventy years. As she gets older, she says, her explanation becomes more simple and more clear. It is men who have determined the social priorities and for many reasons they have turned away from the organic world to the mechanical one.

'We do not know what sort of society women would have shaped,' she said, 'for their contribution has never been allowed' (1982). In 1974, she wrote in *The New Humanist* that 'the astonishing fact of human history is that religion, philosophy, political, social and economic thought have been reserved as the prerogative of men. Our cultural world is the product of male consciousness' (p. 257).

In 1978 I had read a similar statement of Dorothy Smith's where she claimed that we are constantly informed that we have a human society, the product of human effort when what we have is really a *male* society – the product of *male* effort, and this includes the effort to relegate women to an inferior position and to exclude women's values. Ideas, images and themes, she said 'have either been produced by men or controlled by them. Insofar as women's work and experience has been entered into, it has been on terms decided by men and because it has been approved by men. That is why women have had no written history until very recently, no share in making religious thoughts, no political philosophy, no representation of society from their view, no poetic tradition, no tradition in art,' for 'What is there –

spoken, sung, written, made emblematic in art,' what is held up as *our* heritage is none other than a male heritage. Women have been denied a past (p. 282–3).

When I had read these words in 1978 I was so excited: they explained so much, they seemed so new: but these ideas were not new for Dora Russell. For decades she had understood that women were excluded from those areas which men had decided were important, and had therefore monopolised for themselves. And of course before her Elizabeth Cady Stanton, Susan B. Anthony and Matilda Joslyn Gage had understood how and why women were prevented from playing a part in forming our society – which is why in 1881 they had begun to edit a women's version of women's history (*History of Woman Suffrage*). But I did not know of Dora Russell's ideas and she did not know of Stanton's, Anthony's and Gage's; and this in itself helps to show how women are prevented from forming a tradition and constructing a past.

For as long as men have been writing history, women have been making it – and it is very different from men's, argues Dora Russell: while ever men have thought about the way the world should be organised, so too have women – and their plans have been very different from men's. But the only history, the only tradition we are presented with is the male view, and all of women's different priorities and plans, visions and values have been lost; and according to Dora Russell we can no longer afford this. To her it is not just desirable but absolutely necessary that women's way of viewing the world becomes a basis for our society. This has been one of the guiding principles of her life.

She has written her autobiography (*The Tamarisk Tree*, volumes I and II, and volume III is currently being completed) in which she gives the detail of her life and describes and comments on the events of the twentieth century – from a woman's point of view. Seeing the century through women's eyes is in itself a remarkable experience: events look very different when a burning issue of the 1920s is that of making it legal for women to have information on birth control. But seeing the changes through Dora Russell's eyes has an added dimension.

In 1923, after having visited both Russia and America (and China), Dora Russell got a contract to write a book on the implications of industrialism. She had seen the optimism of communism and visited the heartland of capitalism, but not for her was the major male preoccupation of 'which is better?'. It was what both systems had *in common* which for Dora Russell became an overriding issue, for both assumed that technology would solve human problems. It was an assumption she did not share and one that she saw as decidedly dangerous and destructive.

Her view was not understood – certainly not by Bertrand Russell (universally renowned for his powers of comprehension), and not by the intellectuals of the time. As so many women before and since have done, she lost her confidence in her explanation and lost the taste for the task. She wrote *The Right To Be Happy* – as a sort of substitute, she says. But in 1982 the book on industrialism was written – *The Religion of the Machine Age*. For sixty years she had been testing her idea that only men could have invented machines and made a god of them: only men could fail to see that the machine is not the answer to the problems of human existence. Dora Russell's autobiography contains sixty years of observations on men and their machines.

'Ah well,' I said to her, 'you know that I keep saying every fifty years women have to reinvent the wheel. We discover something new but after fifty years have passed it has been lost, and has to be rediscovered again. You put forward your ideas in the 1920s and now, a bit over fifty years later you are putting them forward again.'

'You mean I've lived long enough to come full circle, to be back in fashion again?' she asked me, and then added with a touch of humour and a trace of anger, 'I don't recommend the forty-nine years in between' (1982).

Dora Russell's autobiography is readily available and in it she provides such an extensive and illuminating account of her life that any further documentation – even if space would permit – would be quite superfluous. I could not hope to adequately cover the depth and diversity of her involvement in the many issues aimed at improving the quality of life, so I have decided instead to concentrate more on the ideas which

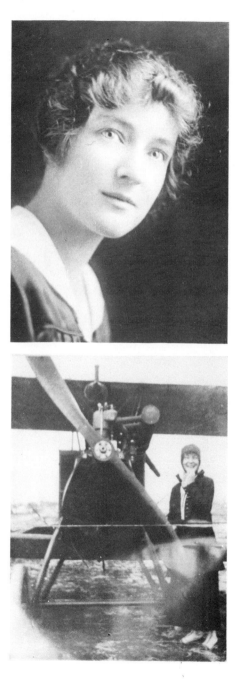

1   Hazel Hunkins
Hallinan—women's rights worker

2   Hazel Hunkins Hallinan
alongside the aeroplane used
when dropping leaflets over San
Francisco

3   Hazel Hunkins Hallinan in 1978, celebrating the 50th anniversary of the vote for women with four Stock Exchange guides (Photographer Frank Martin, *The Guardian*)

4   The young Rebecca West (Photographer E. O. Hoppé, The Mansell Collection)

5 Rebecca West, 1972
(Photographer Reginald Coote,
The Sunday Telegraph)

6 The young Dora Russell whilst
a High School student

7 Dora Russell in 1928

8 Dora Russell during the War Years

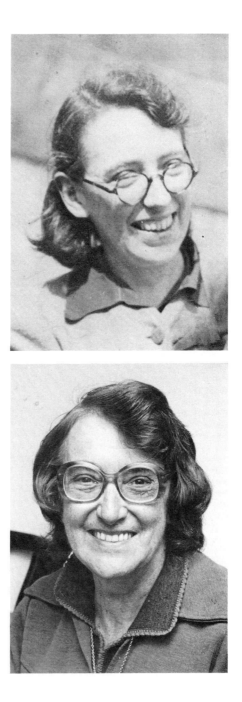

9   Mary Stott in 1943

10   Mary Stott today

11   Mary Stott with Jill Tweedie on an Anti-Discrimination march in Hyde Park, 1971
(Photographer E. Hamilton West, *The Guardian*)

12   Constance Rover in 1943,
aged 33

13   Constance Rover, after the
publication of *Love, Morals and
the Feminists,* 1970

A SKETCH FROM NATURE.

14   From a selection made by Constance Rover for her publication, the *Punch Book of Women's Rights,* that reflected the issues of the times; this gives some idea of women's position in society in the absence of education and economic independence

15   Also from the above selection, this represents a male response – not unknown today (Reproduced by permission of *Punch*)

"EVIL COMMUNICATIONS," &c.

SCENE—*Mrs. Lynn Hunter's Drawing-Room, during a Lecture on "Women's Rights."*

Modest Youth (in a whisper, to Young Lady looking for a Seat). "ER—EXCUSE ME, BUT DO YOU BELIEVE IN THE EQUALITY OF THE SEXES, MISS WILHELMINA?"

Young Lady. "MOST CERTAINLY I DO, MR. JONES."

Modest Youth. "HAW! IN THAT CASE OF COURSE I NEEDN'T GIVE YOU UP MY CHAIR!"

she offers to women today, ideas tested and tempered by her life as a twentieth-century feminist.

Born in 1894 into a middle-class family, Dora Russell had a secure and happy childhood, and a good education at the time – for a girl! She had wanted to go on the stage but somehow or other a scholarship to Girton settled the question of a theatrical life. She knew of course that while women were allowed to attend classes and sit examinations at Cambridge, they were not allowed to get degrees[1] and this severely limited women's job opportunities. Still, there were the classes, the fellow students and there was always teaching – or even the possibility of a fellowship at one of the women's colleges.

Looking back Dora Russell says that she can see that there was always within her the desire to question authority, but before she went to Cambridge – and before World War I – there was really no way to go about it. She accepted the Edwardian principles and customs of her time for want of an alternative frame of reference to check them by or question them in. If there was any great intellectual quest it was in the area of religion.

'It's almost impossible to explain to anyone who didn't experience it, what it was like before 1914,' she said. 'We were leaving behind the Victorian era and were convinced that everything would go on, getting better and better. We couldn't see, and we wouldn't have been able to comprehend what was coming. That enormous crash and carnage. It could never have been visualised, and when it came, it changed us all profoundly and probably permanently. We no longer trusted. We no longer had faith in authority. And we certainly didn't spend our time after that debating the finer points of religious dogma' (1982).

Not that it took World War I to promote a crisis in religious faith in Dora Russell. She had already made a move away from the doctrines of her upbringing when she joined the *Heretics*, not long after her arrival in Cambridge. It was a brave, bold move for a young woman to openly profess her 'heresy'. Apart from meeting on Sunday instead of going to church, a condition of membership was that you didn't accept *authority* – you only accepted those things that were convincing on a rational or scientific basis. This stand has also been one which Dora Russell has maintained throughout her life: she has never been content to accept existing arrangements, never satisfied with the received social wisdom. She has always asked *how* do we know this is so, who says it, and what do they have to gain or lose? And she certainly has never been satisfied when the answer is MEN! In a society where males are the authorities Dora Russell still openly professes her heresy.

Dora Russell traces the origins of many of her beliefs back to 1914–1918, and the years directly after the war. She talks of the confusing conflict which she experienced when she accompanied her civil servant father as his private secretary on his trip to America during the war: the reason for his visit was to persuade the Americans to conserve oil (even then) and to help make it available to the British. She was rather shocked by the habits of some of the Americans she met – she was after all mixing with members of what we would today call 'the industrial-military complex' – and she was deeply distressed when she found that some of those whom she met simply saw war as a source of profit. That they little understood the ravages and destruction of the war in Europe – and that she felt she understood more about the Germans than the Americans, for she was, after all steeped in the study of German philosophy and language – was at first disconcerting. But the experience helped to shape her consciousness and convinced her that war and 'enemies to be conquered' was a stupid and brutal way of explaining and solving human problems.

Before she had left Britain she had become familiar with the name of Bertrand Russell – and not in an academic capacity. In Britain during World War I there was no legal right to be a conscientious objector and any man who refused to fight was seen as a traitor, and treated accordingly: so harsh was the treatment that some men committed suicide. Bertrand Russell was too old for service but he came out publicly in the defence of the younger men and the reception he got made a contribution to Dora's education in politics. Any last vestiges of faith in the good sense and judgment of the authorities was finally destroyed for Dora, when with

friends she joined Bertrand Russell on a walking holiday –
which had to be inland because of the fear expressed by
officials that he would signal enemy ships if he were near the
coast!

The absurd lengths to which a government will go in
time of war, the malpractices that it will engage in, in the
name of national security, was a lesson learnt early by Dora
Russell who has observed again and again throughout the
century the folly and ferocity of war. The conduct of those in
power should always be open to question she argues, and yet
at the time when questions most need to be asked as in time of
war – or preparation for it – those in power often take extraordinary steps to prevent questions from being asked. The
idea that it is other countries which have 'closed' systems of
government, while our own is 'open' is one that she finds
preposterous. She discovered at Bertrand Russell's trial that
the government was not even prepared to be an object of
amusement: as far as Dora is concerned Bertrand Russell's
main crime (for which he got six months – initially to be
served in the Second Division) was not what he said about the
government's thoughts on war, but the fact that he said the
government had no thoughts at all.

Bertrand Russell was transferred, however, to the First
Division, which, says Dora Russell, was most fortunate,
because the only implement he ever knew how to hold was a
pen (and books and writing materials were permitted to First
Division prisoners), and he would not have been a huge
success as a mail-bag-maker. Reared as he had been in an
aristocratic 'charmed circle' he had little or no idea how to
attend to his own human maintenance.

'He didn't know about men sharing the domestic responsibilities?' I asked Dora. 'He wouldn't have taken kindly to
the notion that men should do their own shitwork?'

'No,' she said emphatically, 'he definitely would not. I
suppose you would call him a chauvinist. But he was very
much *for* women's rights' (1982).

Dora and Bertrand Russell got to know each other better,
even though Russell was already married, but separated
from his wife Alys Pearsall-Smith,[2] and had already been
involved in a few affairs. Perhaps if Dora had been aware of

the way he had treated his first wife, she would not have seen it as a propitious omen for her own relationship with Russell. But she was young, full of hope, did not seek marriage, and was a firm believer in the idea that human beings should be able to express their care and concern freely.

When she met Bertrand Russell, Dora was of course a feminist. She was constantly concerned with the elimination of prejudice against her sex and a staunch supporter of women's suffrage and women's rights: Sylvia Pankhurst became a close friend. Confronted daily with the restrictions placed upon women, Dora railed against them and determined to remove them: but if she was concerned with breaking the barriers which prevented women from obtaining degrees, she was equally concerned with breaking the barriers which prevented women from gaining acknowledgment as sexual beings.

There have always been different forms of feminism and this was no less so in the 1920s than it is today.[3] Once women's suffrage was a reality there were – understandably – those feminists who believed that women were the equals of men and who should therefore be able to lead public lives like men, but because society was not arranged for those who led public lives to accept private responsibilities (such as parenting and child care, not to mention other domestic responsibilities) then women who wanted to live like men in 'public' found themselves living very differently from men in 'private'. The *career man* may have been able to return to spouse and family for rest, recreation and replenishment, but the *career woman* rarely if ever had a spouse who provided domestic comforts and harmony to return to.

Men, of course were in the advantageous position of having set up the social arrangements which allowed them a blend of public activity and private service. Women who wanted to demonstrate their equality – and quite a few of them did – found that they had to fit into these social arrangements, for *equality* neither then nor now consisted of being able to formulate their *own* arrangements. Had women been able to design the patterns of public/private life no doubt we would have found a form in which for women, the two are compatible, but women have had no such opportunity with the result that while for men the existing arrangements may be convenient, for women they represent conflict. Because men have stipulated that women are responsible for the daily maintenance of the human species, then men may *work* unfettered, while women must *work*, and *work*: not only do many men have *one* job, while women have *two*, but when men are not at their job they may be having their strength replenished, while women work to replenish it.

Despite what men may decree, women are not stupid. The women in the 1920s who decided to enter the public world were frequently well aware that there were simply not sufficient hours in the day to perform the two jobs required of the 'working' woman. If they were going to undertake the public job they had to forgo the private one. It was work enough to care for themselves at the end of the day (for many of these 'new' women did *not* have other women as servants): it would have been impossible to care for husband – and family.

Many women therefore chose spinsterhood. The prevailing morality which stigmatised and penalised the single mother, and which at the same time made it illegal for women to be provided with information on birth control methods, meant that heterosexual relationships for single working women were virtually impossible. Men have never been confronted with a choice between a job or a woman – on the contrary, one of the most trenchant criticisms of the time was associated with the sexual double standard which permitted to men a job, a wife – and a mistress! Peculiar gifts of insight aren't necessary to see who is making up the rules when men were provided with such options – but for a woman it was often a choice between a job and a man!

Living without a man, was and is a perfectly reasonable although not often understood existence. What distressed Dora Russell was that it was not always a freely chosen one, but an existence forced upon women as a consequence of the arrangements that men had set up for themselves. Heterosexuality was equated with sexuality and while some women may have found it more difficult than others it was nonetheless a requirement that women deny their sexual identity if they wanted to participate in the public world of men. Not only was this rank injustice as far as Dora was concerned, it was destructive.

She was insistent that women should have the right to economic independence – that they should have the right to enter the public world: and she was equally insistent that they should have the right to sexual independence – the right to a sexual identity. She was adamant that the right to economic independence could not be bought by surrendering sexual independence.

Dora Russell is well aware that in a male dominated society, women are exploited: she is well aware that woman are the nurturers in our society and that their nurturing has been exploited. But she refuses to conclude from this that there is something wrong with nurturing! 'Just because men have been able to use it against women, doesn't mean we have to deny it,' she states emphatically (1982).

She genuinely believes that women *are* closer to nature, that because of their child-bearing capacity and their child-rearing role, they do understand more about the organic and inter-related nature of the universe. She is quite content with some of the traditional characteristics attributed to women: what she is not content with is the value that these charac-teristics have been accorded under patriarchy. 'Equality means men coming up to our standards, half the time,' she says. 'It means men meeting our standards of nurturing. It does not mean that we should deny our nurturing, our strength as mothers, to meet theirs!' (1982).

Today, Dora Russell runs the grave risk of being mis-understood, of being equated with biological determinism and all the negative connotations it has acquired. Currently there is a tendency to 'gloss over' the thorny question rather than to bring up – yet again – all the arguments about women's reproductive ability being evidence of disqualifica-tion for any other sort of ability. But if in some ways Dora Russell does go along with the idea that biology is destiny it is by no means a Freudian version of destiny that she has in mind. Regardless of the real risks of misinterpretation – and misrepresentation – she is unrepentant in her assertion that men are biologically different from women, and that the male view of the world, and male consciousness, is different from women's. Women's biology, is to Dora Russell, a strength and not a weakness, something to be celebrated, not denied, something which men do not have: 'Of course men have used this against us,' she says, 'they have used our biology as a reason for keeping us from being educated, for keeping us out of the public world, for declaring our opinions unreliable. But they are wrong and we are fools if we believe them' (1982).

Dora Russell was just as unrepentant when she was critical of some of the feminists of her youth who flushed with hopes at the prospects of entering the male world previously denied them, renounced their female biology, aspired to male values and male consciousness, and claimed that there was no room for love and children in the public world! 'What a denial of our humanity,' she says sadly, 'that at the centres of power, where decisions are made, there is no room for nurturing, for love, and children. There is more to life than the "inhuman" work place. It is terrible that many men do not know that: it is a tragedy if women follow them' (1982).

These are Dora's values now, and they were her values when she met Bertrand. She did not seek marriage. She did want to be financially independent and she did want a sexual identity. She knew she wanted children. Such a philosophy put her outside the realm of social respectability.

'There was all this nonsense about "free love",' she said drily, 'and upright people were terribly afraid of it. It was a term that was used to besmirch people's reputations, it was an insult if you were called a "free lover".' Dora *was* called a free lover – not only because of her relationship with Bertrand Russell but because of her work in the campaign for birth control. ('Any woman who wanted to engage in hetero-sexual activity without accepting the consequences had to be a "loose" woman and a prostitute.') But her philosophy was not to do with permissiveness – as she pointed out to me with some amusement – but was a protest against the sexual slavery, particularly of marriage, which required women to trade their bodies in return for financial support. 'It was *free* love instead of *forced* love we were advocating,' she said, 'where a woman could choose to love instead of being pur-chased for it.' Ruefully, she added, 'It was a matter of quality, not quantity, but there were many people who didn't see it that way, or didn't want to' (1982).

This was the philosophy that Dora brought to her relationship with Bertrand Russell. He was at that stage a well-established academic, in his forties, who was growing every day in public stature (at least in some quarters) with his uncompromising pacifist stand. One can speculate as to whether he was a suitable companion for Dora given that his commitment was to the development of intellect which was free from the fetters of emotion, passion and the clutterings of human fallibility and foibles, when Dora was so intent on using the resources of human consciousness for human ends. It was not long before their different philosophies pushed them to view the same events in very different ways.

At one time they planned to go to Russia together, for in the midst of the dashed dreams and desolation of World War I, the 1917 Revolution held out the promise of a more sane and satisfactory society and they wanted to see it for themselves. But Bertrand was then offered a place on an official delegation, which he thought would provide a better opportunity for gathering information than a private trip. So off he went in an official capacity: Dora decided to make a private visit of her own – and managed it, which was no small feat considering the obstacles that were placed in the way of those wanting to visit Russia.

What she saw made a great impression on her but when she returned, before she really even had time to compare notes, Bertrand Russell asked her to go with him to China. The decision was not an easy one for her to make and the significance of it was never appreciated by Bertrand.

There she was, a young woman in her early twenties just embarking on her life of independence and she was being asked to give it up. She had shown considerable aptitude as a scholar – she had even got one of the fellowships at Girton – and was very interested in her research on the development of eighteenth-century thought. Many of the opportunities for which so many women had fought so long were just beginning to materialise when Bertrand Russell asked her to make the choice between a job and a man. And it was a choice which might not be available again: if giving up a fellowship wasn't 'black mark' enough to prevent her from getting another one, being involved in a public scandal would be. It was also a definite case of putting all her eggs in one basket: what if the relationship with Bertrand Russell did not work? There was no 'inherited wealth' to fall back on, and probably only very precarious means of earning one's living with no reasonable assured university future, and no degree. Bertrand Russell could never understand what it cost Dora to go with him – in some ways it was the end of her dream of how women might live if they had both economic and sexual independence.

On the way to China, however, there was ample time to discuss Russia: it was in the Red Sea that Dora realised that their philosophies were far apart and that Bertrand Russell simply did not understand hers!

The Russia that Dora Russell had seen was one that was just emerging from the medieval period. It was a country where one dogma was being replaced by another, where the religion of Christianity had given way to the religion of Communism. And Dora had rejected religion – with its emphasis on authority and obedience – as a basis for explaining and organising human life. She didn't accept that paradise was some future existence where Jehovah reigned among the chosen and she didn't accept that it was some future existence where the state would just wither away and the whole complexity of human relationships would run like clockwork. For her whole adult life Dora Russell has wanted to know *who* is winding the clock (and she isn't satisfied with mystical explanations), and what happens if the clock breaks down?

Her paradise – which was not some future state – was literally and figuratively a more *earthy* one. In her view human beings were part of the ecological scheme and they possessed rich resources of consciousness and creativity which could be used to construct a society which was ecologically inter-related and which helped to foster consciousness and creativity. It was the *quality* of life which was her prime concern and industrialism – which was the basis of American and English society and which was being taken on in Russia – which emphasised *quantity*, seemed to her to be the complete antithesis to human social organisation.

'Industrialism was the great religion,' she said, explaining to me the philosophy she has adhered to for sixty years; 'Industrialism is the religion with "the machine" as the god going to answer all the prayers. Communism and capitalism were just competing sects. They still are.' And like all religions, they outlaw those who ask awkward questions: the few who raise their voice in protest are heretics.

'One of the problems with industrialism is that it's based on the premise of more and more. It has to keep expanding to keep going. More and more television sets. More and more cars. More and more steel, and more and more pollution,' she added as an aside. 'We don't question whether we *need* any more or what we'll do with them. We just have to keep on making more and more if we are to keep going. Sooner or later it's going to collapse. It could even be happening now' (1982).

To Dora Russell, industrialism is the enemy of human freedom, the end of creativity, liberty, autonomy, or democracy as we know it. 'Industrial societies can only be run successfully by dictators or oligarchs,' she said, and quoted the example of Hitler; 'Look at the way he could efficiently build up a military industrial complex. And look at what we will do to keep industrialism going. What will we be prepared to give up for jobs? Look at what we have done already with the principle of more and more when it comes to nuclear weapons' (1982).

Dora Russell tried to raise this issue in the 1920s but her words fell on deaf ears – Bertrand Russell's among them. To her there is some satisfaction – and some irony – in the fact that those very same words have been revived today – partly for the contribution that they make to the film *Reds*. The film is based on a book by Jack Reed and while Hazel Hunkins Hallinan placed flowers on Reed's grave when she visited Russia, Dora Russell spoke to him in Petrograd when she visited Russia. 'It was just before he died,' she said, 'and we talked at great length about what was happening in Russia. Of all the "witnesses" that were called in the film *Reds*, I was the only one who spoke to Reed on the spot. Not that that made them take me seriously,' she added.

We discussed the film, and her contribution to it. We

commented on the way she was misrepresented and the 'put down', characteristic of patriarchal society, whereby the women witnesses were asked questions about *love* and the men about *politics*. 'That's not to negate love,' said Dora, 'it only proves how men distort it.' She anticipated my every move.

But some of the material she had written during the early days after the Russian Revolution was used in the publicity material for *Reds*. Sixty years is a long time for words to wait before seeing the light of publication. Dora could not get her views printed at the time – not even in the relatively radical pages of the *Liberator* edited by Crystal Eastman and her brother. Those who were 'pro' the Russian Revolution did not take kindly to criticisms of it. And Dora's writing *was* critical. 'But there was one advantage of not being published,' she said, 'for I didn't ever get involved in the debates about communism versus capitalism. As I think it's a complete waste of time – because really, they are just two sides of the same machine coin, at least I wasn't distracted by that issue' (1982).

But there were other issues to distract her. In China, Bertrand Russell nearly died and Dora became pregnant, and the two events are not unrelated. Dora Russell has talked at length of some of the intellectuals of her time and the energy they put into suppressing their emotions – so that their intellects could remain pure and free from passion. Her analysis leads her to believe that one of the side effects of such 'discipline' is partial impotency and she can quote quite a lengthy and impressive list of emotion-free intellectuals who were unable to summon emotion when needed. That Bertie was almost delirious and no longer either willing or able to suppress his feelings is how Dora accounts for her pregnancy.

Bertrand Russell survived (partly because of Dora's excellent nursing – another feature of women's nurturance) and they returned to England, where he immediately per-suaded his wife, Alys, of the necessity of a divorce. The unborn child could be a boy, and a legitimate heir if Bertrand were married to Dora.

This must have been an immense blow for Alys who had wanted children but who had been persuaded by Bertrand that it would be unwise. Nevertheless she agreed to the quickest divorce that was possible. But it was also a blow to Dora who was now required – in the interest of patriarchal legitimacy – to marry. Being the wife of a member of the aristocracy was not the independent life she had aspired to.

'Despite the fact that Bertie assured me I would never be required to grace the head of his table,' said Dora, 'that was precisely what he wanted' (1982).

The newly married couple lived in Chelsea and rather than finding that all her dreams had come true upon her marriage, Dora Russell found that many of her problems had just begun. We talked about 'Bertie's expectations' – and requirements – and she indicated a distinct reluctance to 'show up Bertie', displaying a far more generous attitude to him, than he did to her. But as he has been portrayed so positively by himself and others, I feel under no obligation to perpetuate such a tradition.

Yes, Dora Russell agreed, Bertie did demand all the creature comforts without putting effort into establishing them; yes, he did think his work was more significant, that women were less intelligent and that the world should revolve around him; yes, he did feel quite secure and he did require her to give up her friends of her own age group; yes, she did become something of an appendage, the mother of his child and the pourer of tea at social gatherings: but at the same time he was very different from most other men, he was an ardent campaigner for women's rights, he did stand for parliament on a women's suffrage platform, and he was prepared to support her in any work she was able to take on.

There have been other women who have been involved with men who in public are champions of women's rights, and 'model' husbands, and who in private are firmly committed to men's rights and this has been the source of some discomfort – even conflict – for the women. Lucy Stone, for example, a nineteenth-century American feminist who was married to Henry Blackwell, seemed to have difficulty reconciling the demands made on her as a wife with her husband's public persona which was above reproach within the women's movement: who would appreciate her grievance? Charlotte Perkins Gilman nearly went mad with her 'loving husband'

(Walter Stetson), who engendered enormous feelings of guilt and inadequacy in her which were only 'explained' – and exorcised – in her fictional account of the loving husband who very nearly killed his wife with 'understanding' in *The Yellow Wallpaper* (1898). Did Dora Russell feel the same way?

No doubt it would have been extremely difficult to challenge the world's champion of women's rights about his domestic habits: such discussion would have hardly warranted consideration as a serious political issue. As Dora Russell firmly states one of the life-long battles has been to break down men's definition of *politics*, but there is little evidence that for Bertrand Russell politics began at home. Had Dora Russell tried to make an issue out of the unjust division of labour – or even of the more subtle pressure which required that she take 'second place', then if she hadn't been decried for 'complaining' she would probably have been dismissed as 'incredible'. There is often a real dilemma for women who have relationships with 'enlightened' and supportive men whose commitment to women's rights is considered beyond criticism.

Yet while Bertrands' career progressed and expanded, while his esteem was enhanced and his identity confirmed, Dora Russell's individual identity was undermined and her opportunities for paid work were diminished. The university was no longer open to her and although there was still the appeal of the stage, it wasn't a feasible option given that she had to bear the brunt of domestic responsibilities. Bertrand Russell's requirements were not only considerable – they were constant: he didn't leave home each day for regular hours at the office as Crystal Eastman found when she arrived to interview Dora and had to do so in the presence of Bertrand (see Spender, 1982b, pp. 476–7). Even a comparable life to the one which Bertie led as intellectual and writer was not possible for Dora – and not just because time would not permit but because when she put forward *her* ideas there was generally the strong (patriarchal) assumption that she had simply been listening to Bertie! This was not an ideal setting in which to bloom! For all women there is the difficulty of confounding the well-entrenched belief of a male dominated society that women cannot be creative and original thinkers (with those who show their competence in men's terms accorded the arrogant 'put-down' of having 'masculine minds') but for the wife of Bertrand Russell, required to live in his intellectual shadow, the problem was intensified.

It was but a few years since Dora had envisaged for herself a life of liberty and love and she found herself instead sharing the common and traditional fate of many women – she was an 'interrupted' wife and mother who sincerely wanted to meet the needs of those whom she loved but who found that they could only be fulfilled at the expense of meeting her own. 'It's a conflict women have to face and yet it isn't necessary,' she said. 'It wouldn't be such a challenge to organise society so that women can be mothers, lovers, nurturers – and also lead active and meaningful lives in a public sense. But it hasn't been done' (1982).

'Men's values and priorities are so obvious,' Dora Russell declared. 'They have reduced everything to economics and they cannot or will not see that there is so much more to life than measuring work, skill and money. They have taken "work" and "politics" and pushed women into developing and maintaining the social and human functions, and yet both sexes need some of both areas. It's so simple really. It's what Alexandra Kollontai was trying to tell them in 1920,' she said, quoting her favourite feminist, 'and it's what I've been saying since 1920, but they didn't hear her and they didn't hear me' (1982).

Unlike many of my own generation who were divided from feminists of the past, Dora Russell has not felt an absence of female models. For her, Alexandra Kollontai stands out as a beacon, a woman whose words of wisdom Dora Russell heard in Russia and whose path she has followed ever since.

'If Alexandra Kollontai hadn't been a women, then many today would know about her and what she tried to do,' Dora Russell said sadly, 'She was the only woman in Lenin's government and the only one who could see that there was a new way of bringing together nurturing for men, work for women, and compatability between the sexes. But she got pushed out then and she's been pushed out ever since and she's never been given her due.'

In Dora Russell's view, Alexandra Kollontai faced all the age-old problems. In 1980, she wrote of her that: 'Kollontai, often alone, faced virtually every problem of a woman seeking her rights, whether as an individual or as a sex: the lover who sees woman only as a sex-object; the male (or female) politician to whom feminism is a tiresome bourgeois red-herring in the path of socialism – not to mention the thousand and one arguments about women's lack of education, inferior physical strength, or mind, and the rest' (p. 460). And there were the problems of trying to organise society so that women were not solely and exclusively responsible for the rearing of children – when a woman who said that there must be more than domestic responsibilities was branded as irrational. 'In revolt against the rights of possession of wives and children enjoyed by men, to her, . . . responsibilities for the care of mothers and children rested on the whole community. This did not mean as (her) enemies contended, the cold hearted takeover of children by the state. In fact, the problem of family versus state is still unsolved in industrial societies today' (p. 460).

In her early married life when Dora Russell encountered some of the restrictions placed upon women in a male dominated and male-oriented world she was not unaware of the source of the problem and she must have often recalled her experience with Alexandra Kollontai: 'In the same year, 1920, as I stood beside Kollantai in the great Women's Congress in the Bolshoi theatre in Moscow, I expressed in an article my misgivings about the machine age; my fears that communists and socialists, stressing economics to the exclusion of less materialist values, would end up as nothing but capitalists themselves. Perhaps Kollontai and I shared the same misgivings; perhaps the same dreams' (1980, p. 461).

What Dora Russell most certainly did share with Alexandra Kollontai was a similar rebuff when she tried to inform socialist men – in Britain – that there was more in life for them than materialism, machines, and work, and more in life for women than maternity.

Despite the constraints of being Mrs Bertrand Russell, Dora did find purposeful and affirming work and it was in the campaign for birth control. Most women during the early 1920s were relatively ignorant when it came to matters of contraception[4] but at least for middle-class and educated women there was the possibility of obtaining a book (such as the one written by Marie Stopes, 1918). Books, however, were beyond the reach of working-class and uneducated women. Because of this, a pamphlet by Margaret Sanger which was expressly written (with diagrams) in a form which working-class women could understand, was published in 1923 and sold cheaply, virtually on street corners.

The pamphlet was declared obscene and was seized.

Although she knew there was no chance of winning an appeal, Dora Russell nevertheless organised one, partly to bring to public attention the bald fact that there was a way for women to prevent conception but men would not permit women to know about it. (It must be remembered that at this time the policy of the Ministry of Health was 'to threaten with dismissal doctors or health visitors who gave . . . advice [on birth control] as well as indicating that grants to health centres might be withheld' Russell, 1977, p. 170.) The appeal was lost, but not before the magistrates were alarmed, according to Dora Russell. 'It was bad enough that women might be able to find a way to defy the so-called natural order and have sex without babies, but what was even worse,' said Dora with undisguised glee, 'was that such a pamphlet might come into the hands of their wives, who would read the astonishing statement that it was perfectly reasonable for a woman to expect to enjoy sexual intercourse. This was a new idea for many women and it brought with it another one: if they were not enjoying sex, then what could be wrong with their husbands? No wonder so many men were intent on suppressing that pamphlet' (1982).

'You can't just look at women's progress in terms of laws and acts, in the areas which men control,' Dora Russell reminded me. 'You have to look at the area of relationships, where women have been influential, and there you will see that there have been enormous changes. It's not so long since the majority of men believed that women's only function was to be pregnant – some of the men were in the Labour Party. They genuinely believed that women's duty was to go forth and multiply in penance and pain, and their whole universe was turned upside down at the prospect of women making decisions about when they would have children, how many they would have, and under what conditions they would have them. And the very idea that women should have anything other than a *dutiful* attitude towards sexual intercourse was just too much for them. So many men thought they were having their power taken away from them. They felt worried and cheated – emasculated!' (1982).

'Some of them still do,' I said. 'One of the classic male responses to women's greater freedom is to accuse women of emasculating them, of taking away some of their power,' and I quoted some authoritative sources – from Freud onwards. 'It says a lot about men though that they can feel deprived, cheated of their dues, if they have to surrender some of their power over women. But I'm one of those who believe they never should have had such power in the first place, so I'm all for emasculation – but we'd better not tell the press. They'd have a field day.'

'When you put it like that,' said Dora Russell, 'I'm for it as well – though as a feminist I've spent years and years trying to persuade people that I'm not anti-men, that I'm not out to cheat or destroy men. It's an awful burden when you want change so much – when the whole society needs change so much – but you are not supposed to come out openly and say so. If I say "Look at that man – he's a destroyer" – and there are a lot of men on the television I want to say that about, then I become the one who's in the wrong. *He* gets the sympathy and *I* get the sarcasm for being such a terrible woman. It's an issue men have sorted out quite well among themselves. The Tories can say dreadful things about the Labour Party, and vice versa, the Labour Party can call the Tories *destroyers* without terrible personal things being said about them, but it's not allowed in the politics and struggles between the sexes. It's women who are made responsible for men's pride and it's women who are blamed when it's undermined. I learnt that lesson well when I was young,' she said. 'There were so many men who thought their masculine pride and privilege was being taken away from them at the mere suggestion of birth control' (1982) and she went on to relate some of the 'highlights' of the campaign.

From Dora Russell's point of view it was patently clear that when it came to birth control, working-class women were going to be the *last* to know about it, when they were likely to be the women with the greatest need to know about it as they tried to support large families on low wages, and so she took her case to working-class men, to the Labour Party and socialists. But she didn't get much satisfaction and was bluntly informed that it was not *less* children that the working class needed, but *more* money. 'They wouldn't even recognise my argument that if a woman lived in Buckingham Palace and had all the money she needed she still wouldn't want a baby each year' (1982). (We both decided that this argument might need to be revised in the near future.)

While Dora was being admonished for bringing sex into politics (and accused of trying to split the Labour Party over this 'ridiculous' issue) she was busily and defiantly trying to introduce politics into sex as she again and again pointed out that it was men – *who did not bear children* – who were making the rules about child bearing. She also helped to coin a slogan that spelt out this message loud and clear:

IT IS FOUR TIMES AS DANGEROUS TO BEAR A CHILD AS TO WORK IN A MINE: AND MINING IS MAN'S MOST DANGEROUS TRADE

Great efforts were being made by men to remedy the scandalous practices of mining and to make it more safe: why would men not make the same effort for women? Why indeed did they deliberately oppose measures to make maternity safer for women?

'The men couldn't argue that women were content as they were and didn't want birth control information,' said Dora, 'because the women made such a protest. They were outraged that the men said they couldn't have it. It was astonishing to hear so many women who had been told that the most noble thing they could do was to have babies, fiercely denying that they wanted babies – every year' (1982).

This confrontation with male politics helped to form Dora Russell's attitude to the party-political and parliamentary system. Her experience which began then but which has continued over the decades suggested to her that when men *did* create a small space for women within the political party it was more with a view to containing women rather than providing them with a power base. 'The women's organiser in the Labour Party,' she said, 'wasn't there to help women state the case for birth control to the men, she was there to make sure she put men's case to the women. She tried to make us give up the issue – it wasn't the place, birth control was a private matter. You know all the old arguments that are used. Anything that relates to women is always a "private" matter as far as men are concerned. But it really was a question of men's politics versus women's politics when it came to birth control, and on that issue, *women won*' (1982).

Dora Russell has no great faith in the present parliamentary system. She perfectly understands women's reluctance to participate: 'Parliament,' she states unequivocally, 'is a man's game. It's a substitute for civil war and duelling. It's based completely on the idea of *conflict*. You have to be party *adversaries*. There has to be *opposition*. If one party chooses one thing in its platform, the other party has to show it's different, it has to oppose it. Have you ever heard of anything so ridiculous?' she asked me.

'Politicians will even toe the party political line when it goes against their own conscience. And they'll come out and tell you about it, as if it's understandable! Of course women can't see the sense of such a system, and that's why a lot of them stay out of it. Women like having consensus but the whole parliamentary system is arranged to *prevent* that' (1982).

I reminded her that many of the parliamentary bills which have related to women have often confounded party divisions and have been 'free' or 'conscience' votes (suffrage, abortion, etc.) 'Of course,' Dora Russell replied, 'men have got their own choices sorted out. They have been doing it a long time. They know all about work, and machines, money and markets, and there is a sort of dogma which dictates the way each party goes. But they haven't worked out any schemes on women's issues. They just lump them altogether as *private*, and you wouldn't be a very sensible person if you joined an organisation that thought your politics and priorities were just a matter of personal choices, a matter of conscience. And women are sensible people – that's why they can see there's no place for them in party politics' (1982).

As Dora Russell related some of the skirmishes she has had with 'male politics' it became very clear that the feminist fight in the political arena has been a very long and arduous one. 'Every inch has been a struggle,' she said, 'and there are still many more miles to go.' And in her eyes we haven't always followed the straight road but have wandered up a few 'dead ends' on the way.

One 'gain' that she questions is directly associated with birth control: it is a by-product which she maintains was not foreseen and is still not fully understood. In her analysis of the male view of the world and its origins she comes back to the biological differences between the sexes. 'Before birth control, only for men was there a division between sexual intercourse and the birth of a human being,' she says. 'For men, sexual gratification and conception are virtually the same act and are quickly over. Men can find gratification and can walk away. They can despise themselves for their weakness, despise the woman on whom they were temporarily dependent. They don't have to think again about the relationship between their own body and the next generation. They can have,' she added, 'what I call "a flight from the body" for they can deny their links with growth, with life, with the universe and set off on some scheme of conquest. They can practise a dualism of mind and matter, where they are able to divorce themselves from matter, from the body, from the cycles of life-giving and nurturing' (1982). And there can be no doubt that Dora Russell thinks that this life-denying capacity which she sees as characteristic of male values, has been the basis of our society and the source of destruction.

'It wasn't like that for women before birth-control,' she said. 'For women, sexual intercourse, and the rhythms and experiences of life giving were not two separate activities.

Sexual gratification may have been the end of *one* physical process but it could also be the beginning of *another* – a new process that went on for nine months – and years more,' she added, reminding me that her eldest son still lives with her.

'Sex does signify different things to women and men – or, at least it did before birth control. Of course women should be able to control their own bodies, I have spent my life trying to make sure they are in a position to do so. But when we started we didn't realise that it could be the beginning of women "taking sex like a man". We didn't know it could launch the "sex as entertainment industry", where both sexes could cut themselves off from the living and caring symbolism of sex' (1982).

Dora Russell didn't mean that in order to be a proper woman, one should have children. (I asked her – quite defensively I think!) And she didn't mean that sex should only be for reproduction. All her life she has resisted both these limited definitions of sex as well. But she did mean that sex has become a whole new game since both women and men have been able to dissociate it from nurturing and life-giving. 'There's a lot more sex these days, but I think there's a lot less love,' she said.

In stating her views about sex Dora Russell shows considerable courage. This is not surprising as she has displayed this same indomitable spirit for more than sixty years. She has lived too long, she says, to be swayed by the popularity of a particular belief; she has seen too many ideas come and go – and come again – to be influenced by the latest fashion. She is well aware that her understanding about sex might be mocked and misrepresented but this is not a new position for her to be in, nor is it for her a reason for keeping quiet.

The present frame of values makes it very easy to dismiss as a prude someone who questions the benefits of sex as entertainment – but then, so many women who have questioned the prevailing orthodoxy about sex have been derided as prudish, from Josephine Butler who fought against the policing of 'prostitutes', Christabel Pankhurst who exposed the prevalence of venereal disease in men, to current campaigners against pornography. If you accept – as Dora

Russell does – that most of the values of society are male-determined values, and this most definitely in the case of sexual behaviour, then it seems that the term 'prude' is given to women who resist the prevailing interpretations of suitable sexuality provided by men. To Dora Russell, it does not seem therefore such a bad thing to be called 'prudish'.

Since the introduction of the 'sex as entertainment industry' both women and men are obliged to be extremely enthusiastic about sex as an end in itself, argues Dora Russell. 'Sex is held out as something everyone should have, and there's a lot of pressure on people to buy, and to keep buying. And if you don't want the packaged product that's for sale, you may not just be called a prude: you are likely to have your sanity questioned' (1982).

Dora Russell is in the position of being able to remember what it was like when women were not supposed to find sex pleasurable, when their duty was to submit to their husbands and to be perpetually pregnant. They were not the good old days, and she doesn't want them back. She campaigned against the cruelty and injustice of the arrangements, she wrote books, gave talks, addressed meetings, and helped to bring about change. But today, she also feels a sense of loss when it comes to the value of sexuality in the permissive age, for sex is no longer necessarily a symbol of care, concern and love. It is not love which is freely given but a form of commercial entertainment and for Dora Russell this is another expression of our fundamental loss of human understanding and compassion, another sign of our divorce from the feelings of tending and caring.

When she entered the fray to fight for women's sexual rights, this was an outcome she did not foresee. In 1925, while involved in the campaign for birth control (and involved in domestic responsibilities) she nevertheless found time to write a short book (under the name of Mrs Bertrand Russell at the publisher's request) entitled *Hypatia or Woman and Knowledge*.[5] It is an excellent commentary on the state of play between the sexes at the time.

The preface reveals Dora Russell's knowledge and assessment of women's treatment in the past: 'Hypatia was a university lecturer, denounced by church dignitaries and torn to pieces by Christians,' she writes, and 'Such will probably be the fate of this book: therefore it bears her name.' The first few pages of *Hypatia* reveal her assessment of women's treatment in the present and she makes the point that little has changed.

She begins with the story of Jason and Medea and brings the ancient myth up to date: 'Medea, driven mad – like so many able and remarkable women – by the contempt and ingratitude of men as individuals or in the mass, and aware that the law was a mockery where she was concerned, expressed herself in savage protest after the manner of a militant suffragette. While I can open my newspaper today and read of mothers desperate with hunger, misery, or rage, drowning themselves and their children, I cannot bring myself to look upon Medea as some elemental being from a dark and outrageous past. As for Jason he never did appear to anybody as other than an ordinary male' (1925, p. 2).

'We have a long history of men sacrificing their children with impunity,' said Dora Russell, 'in the name of various causes, for religion, for war, or even for family honour. But if ever a woman – who gave them life – takes it away, it becomes a horror story, not a glorious state.'

'That fits with what so many women have said about patriarchy,' I replied. 'It's where men own all the resources including human resources,' and I quoted Matilda Joslyn Gage and Charlotte Perkins Gilman. 'Women don't own anything, not even their own children so it's an offence against male property when women take the lives of their children, and it's not an offence when men do it.'

Male behaviour has been so outrageously unjust and cruel that in Dora Russell's opinion women have an absolute moral duty to oppose and resist it. There was no choice as far as women were concerned but to begin the sex war in the attempt to get rid of male tyranny, and in *Hypatia* she argued that the 'modern' woman shared much in common with her ancient foremothers: 'We made our just demands and were met with ridicule,' she wrote, chronicling the events of the nineteenth- and early twentieth-century women's move-ment. 'We followed with abuse – all the pent-up anger, misery and despair of centuries of thwarted instinct and intelligence. Man retaliated with rotten eggs. We replied with smashed windows; he with prison and torture. . . . It was a disgraceful exhibition and would not have come to a truce so soon, but that it was eclipsed by the still more disgraceful exhibition of the European War. In 1918 they bestowed the vote (on older women who were deemed less rebellious) just as they dropped about a few Dames and M.B.E.'s as a reward for our services in helping the destruction of our offspring,' and, she adds bitingly, had we killed them ourselves, as Medea did, the *logical* male would have been outraged! (p. 3–4).

Open warfare may have been prohibited after the vote, declared Dora Russell but all that meant was that men took to sniping: women were 'sniped' out of their jobs, cheated of employment, payment, insurance and, she said, summing up the relationship between the sexes in the early 1920s, 'man seeks by every means in his power to drive women back to matrimonial dependence and an existence on less than half a miserably inadequate income; and then he mocks at her when she claims the right to stem the inevitable torrent of children' (p. 5).

It is not so long since I accepted the version of women's history which had the women's movement collapsing either at the outbreak of World War I, or not long after the war, when (older) women got the vote and returned contentedly and meekly to their homes. I was ready to endorse the idea that like women's political activity itself, the introduction of sex into mainstream politics was an aberration and that after World War I it was 'back to normal' as women returned to their domestic duties and the political arena was once more devoted to serious issues of economic and foreign policy. Yet here in 1925 was Dora Russell writing her devastating denunciation of patriarchy and expressing considerable disbelief when many men offered the soothing solution that if women would only be good, all would be well: 'There is too much evidence at present that man professing friendship and concern, is still ready to snatch from us what little we have won' (p. 19). And as for sexual politics being but a passing perturbation in male politics – the idea was preposterous. True, she said, 'the politician has yet to be found who will realise that the sex problem is as fundamental to politics as the class war – and more fundamental than foreign trade and imperial expansion' (p. 4), but all this proved was that politicians had a lot to learn. And learn they would!

In the interest of creating a more humane and sane society, Dora Russell has been an active feminist for more than sixty years. And her ideas, which have been consistent throughout and which she put forward in the 1920s are once again being discussed. Yet because many of us today knew little or nothing about her (for decades her books have been out of print and for many years she was not published) we had thought such ideas were new – even that we had invented them.

Over the years she has been a witness to the male propaganda designed to keep woman in her proper place – serving man – and she can tell many a wry story about the inducements to get women into the workforce – out of the workforce – and then in again, as they are required to adapt to male economic policies and priorities. She well understands that women have very few rights when it comes to some of the more intangible liberties, and that it is men for whom society is arranged, so that woman's duty is to 'fit in' to accommodate male needs. She has been a keen observer of the process that keeps the male at the centre of social concern while women hover around the periphery.

Like Hazel Hunkins Hallinan and Rebecca West, Dora Russell understands the significance of the 'bad press' that women receive and is adamant that this is no accident. In 1925 she made the point which has been for me a relatively recent discovery, that while feminists may be responsible and reasonable in their assessment of men, they will rarely obtain a public hearing (and even more rarely will be attended to) but 'anybody who has anything abusive to say of women, whether ancient or modern, can command a vast public in the popular press and a ready agreement from the average publisher' (1925, p. 6).

A male dominated society is built on the practice of praising men and discrediting women. This is one way to maintain the image of men as the superior sex. It is a form of propaganda identified and discussed by Dora Russell in the

1920s, which permeates the media and which plays an important role in women's subordination, for it diminishes the
stature of women in general and it also works to intimidate
individual women. When the woman who comes out in
defiance of male domination is ridiculed or reviled, it takes
enormous courage to make a stand. Dora Russell has always
shown that courage: she has always made that stand.

Dora Russell doesn't seem to have deluded herself about
the contempt in which women are held in our society. In 1949
Simone de Beauvoir put forward the revolutionary idea that
while men were the representative sex, women were 'other',
while men were defined as in the right, women were defined
as in the wrong, but twenty years *before* Dora Russell had
written with anger and accuracy about women being in the
wrong: she could see that men could disclaim the responsibility for their own actions by blaming women for all the
problems of society.

Women are blamed for ruining the old way of life she
wrote in *Hypatia*, for the industrial revolution ('we let
weaving, spinning, milling and baking go out of our hands', p.
9), and for the degeneration of the species. We are still in the
image of Eve, the scapegoat, Dora Russell argued, for when it
comes to the evils and ills of society there is no doubt that in
men's minds the true culprit is Woman! 'A thousand voices
cried her down – she hadn't enough children; she had too
many; she was an ape; she was a dressed up doll; she was a
Puritan; she was an immoral minx; she was uneducated; they
had taught her too much. Her pinched waist was formerly
abused – now it was her slim and boyish body. Eminent
surgeons committed themselves to the view that the boyish
figure . . . would be the ruin of the race, that race which had
been superbly undegenerate through four centuries of
armour-plate corset and eighteen inch waists' (p. 11). No
matter what women do, argued Dora Russell, women will be
wrong because it is male consciousness that sets the standards and in it, men are in the right!

Reading Dora Russell's books which were published in
the 1920s (and fifty years later in the seventies) and talking
to her about her ideas, it becomes impossible to think of the
women's movement as new. 'What do you think of today's

feminists?' I asked her and she replied good naturedly and with amusement, 'Oh, they're marvellous. But some of them do tend to think they started it all and at times can be quite dismissive of women like me. They've been too ready to believe the male propaganda and to see feminists of earlier generations as bourgeois women, all proper and respectable. And it just wasn't like that at all!' (1982).

I would like to be able to convey some of the joy I found in Dora Russell, to make public my sense of gratitude for the personal contribution she has made to my life. This wonderful woman of eighty-eight whose compassion and humour are so abundant. A woman who had much to be suspicious of when it came to interviewers who wanted to ask her about her life, but who took me into her home, gave me hours and hours of her time ('and time is precious when you are eighty-eight'), entertained me, warmed me, stimulated me and teased me ('Your trouble is you don't think enough. You take too much for granted without thinking about the politics'). She gave me something very precious for I have often wondered what I will be like as an old lady – and now, at least, I have a vision of what one *can* be like.

I spent days sitting by a fire, looking out over parts of Cornwall, while Dora Russell sat at the desk which has been hers for decades. She was writing another book – she had just written two articles and announced the morning I arrived, 'I've just written to the Queen about this disgraceful idea of Reagan addressing parliament.' (Her son *is* Lord Russell, perhaps the letter reached its destination.) Editors of newspapers and magazines also get their fair share of protest letters – although, needless to say, Dora Russell does not get her fair share of publication!

As we talked she referred to things she had written, and with the same ease and familiarity quoted words from 1927 and 1977. In her study and in her presence there was a feeling of continuity, of security. She has lived this way for more than sixty years: she has been talking and writing this way for more than sixty years. Those of us who follow in her footsteps have a familiar not an unknown path to tread.

If I went ostensibly as the interviewer I also found myself answering many questions. I wanted to know about her life as a feminist but it is characteristic of her that she was just as interested in knowing about my life. I wanted her view of the feminism of the earlier part of the century and she wanted my view of the feminism of the seventies and eighties. It was a very lively discussion and even while we were swapping stories I was aware of the unusual nature of our exchange. How often have women been comparing notes on feminism across fifty years? How often are we given the concrete evidence of our heritage and able to see that we are part of a long tradition?

One area she wanted to know more about was political lesbianism. 'There's nothing new about lesbianism,' she said, 'but to me it has sometimes seemed more reactionary than radical. It has been a response to male dominance, to an absence of power, even to segregation. What do you think all those women were doing in harems? Do you think they didn't discover the pleasure of each other? But', she added searchingly, 'do you think that was a free choice or something that was forced upon them?'

'Well, the political lesbians today aren't living in harems,' I said, 'and the reason the term political is used is to make the point that it is a *choice*, that it's sexual politics, and a choice to not have men.'

'Aha,' she said, 'it's a strike. Now that I can understand! And of course women have been doing that for a long time too – right back to Lysistrata. It's a very powerful tool. One of the things it does is deprive men of children.' She was quiet for a while and then added, 'But it deprives women of children too.'

'You,' I said, 'take too much for granted,' unable to resist the temptation of disclosing that all is not what it seems, and I launched into a discussion of the magic of Artificial Insemination Devices (even self-help kits) and the marvels of sperm banks. We had a wantonly wicked half hour where we discussed all the rules that men had made up to protect themselves and which so many women quietly ignored. The rules about legitimacy ('I once spent an evening with some very respectable women who during the course of the conversation revealed that unbeknown to their husbands they each had a child that wasn't their husband's'); rules about abortion ('all those women who for centuries have been helping each other, and who are doing it again today, without either the know-ledge or sanction of men') and rules about the necessity for every woman to have a man ('self-help kits? Really?'). And we talked about all the women who have said it's just so much easier to live with a woman; Crystal Eastman had said it was the only way women could be sure of having the housework shared.

'That's another argument for political lesbianism,' I said, 'you don't have to housetrain women. And it can take so long and be so wearying to housetrain a man. And besides, as you have pointed out, women so often share the same value system, they understand about nurturing, about conserving, patching and mending relationships, that it can be more rewarding to live with a woman who reciprocates than with a man who doesn't even acknowledge the existence of emo-tional management. Sometimes it can just be too much of an issue to explain women's value system to a man in a way that he can understand and see as important.'

But we soon sobered up. 'What an indictment of human relations,' Dora Russell said, and with a feeling verging on despair asked, 'Isn't there any other way? Must we forever go on fighting, trying to rid ourselves of male power and its abominable consequences? Can't men see that they are destroying themselves, us, the planet, the species? Is there no way for us to live in cooperation and harmony, with each other, our fellow human beings, our fellow creatures?' Dora Russell is a pacifist and that pacifism is all-encompassing.

In the 1920s she believed that the only way to peaceful coexistence of the sexes was through education. Not the sort of competitive, life-denying education of the time but through new and creative ways of teaching the young. She and Bertrand Russell started a school (this period of her life is the focus of the second volume of her autobiography) which was not only an opportunity for developing better educa-tional practices, but was also for Dora a chance to combine the private and public roles of a woman: without conflict she could be both a mother and a worker.

Never has Dora Russell subscribed to the idea that women should have the same education as men for the simple reason that it is her opinion that the education system which men designed for themselves is destructive. Her objections which she voiced in the 1920s, and which require little or no modification today are based on the belief that the entire education system shows the way men have divided the world into mind and matter, in western society, and have decided that mind is far more important than matter. To Dora Russell this is an absurd and anti-human 'split' which lies at the root of many of our problems today. She can see *how* it has happened (her forthcoming book, *The Religion of the Machine Age*, traces the process) and she can see *why* men turned away from the body to the intellect, and she can also see how terrible have been the consequences.

'Men have believed that education means education of but one human resource, what they call the intellect,' she said, 'and they have tried so hard to cultivate a state they see as "pure reason" which for them means getting rid of all the clutter and distractions of *feelings*. But human beings *are* feelings, *are* emotions, and we should be educating this, not denying it' (1982).

Training the 'intellect' has been man's way of rising above and mastering the physical world, of establishing his dominion over women and nature. The physical world, women, even his own body he has seen as something to be used, not as something to be nurtured reasons Dora Russell. In this sense she describes male consciousness as cut off from life, from the organic and inter-related nature of existence. That is why he can so readily destroy – relationships, other human beings, the environment. They are not *part* of him, he does not *identify* with them (and Dora Russell insists that women's consciousness does identify with life-giving, with nature, with other human beings, with the totality of the environment); they simply exist to *serve* him.

'When men first began to use reason,' wrote Dora Russell in 1965, 'to study mathematics and the universe about them, they found in this an escape from servitude to their biological existence, even by means of God and religion, the hope of escape from individual death. Women, because of men's sexual needs were always associated with the animal side of men's natures. In between moments of sexual excitement women did not exist for men who then felt themselves the cool, rational, spiritual beings which they aspired to become' (p. 299).

Feeling cool, rational or spiritual is of course no less an emotional state than feeling warm, responsive and physical: preventing oneself from experiencing certain feelings is no less an emotional existence than allowing oneself the experience. Men's so called intellectual existence is just another variation of emotion, though it's a very different form of emotion and feeling to the one they assign women and to which they attach a very different value.

It seems that the emotional existence cultivated by men relies heavily upon repression and denial and is readily threatened – or contaminated – by the emotions and feelings of women. That's why there is a long tradition among men of keeping women out of the way, according to Dora Russell. This is a very different view of male bonding (and a view which is not nearly so flattering) but it is one which Dora Russell has held for many years. Men, she says, have seen themselves at risk with women's values (and the values of the natural world) and have even thought they would be polluted by the presence of women: this belief flows through Judaism and Christianity – and many other religions – where woman is the symbol of evil and a reason for male celibacy. Men have felt it necessary to isolate themselves from women, from human creation, from the rhythms of life and the feelings of nurturance, so that they can protect themselves and their pursuit of pure reason. And this is the basis of the education system.

'Such is the fear of women that it has been, by tradition, essential to a man's education that he should from an early age be removed from feminine influence – sons were taken from their mothers to begin a process of hardening for knighthood, or to go to the monastery for learning: at a later date we find the young hustled off to prep school' (1965; pp. 290–1). And then men have secluded themselves at the workplace and in their social life: they have formed their clubs – working men's clubs, gentlemen's clubs, sporting clubs – in order that they will not be weakened by women's influence. It was 'women's influence' which was missing in education and society, and it was precisely women's influence that was needed, argued Dora Russell to restore the values of life and humanity to our world.

'What men have forgotten and what they don't want to know is that we *are* animals,' says Dora Russell, 'and if we have a purpose it is an ecological one in the here and now. But so many men are repulsed by that idea of being part of, and not superior to the organic world. When I said that we were animals and should start to see ourselves in that light, T. S. Eliot said I was a disgrace and not fit to be teaching children' (1982).

Her book *The Right to be Happy* (1927) is very much an account of human beings as animals where she defies the negative meaning of animal and makes it something very positive and joyous. In 1982 she still held to this thesis – although she admitted that she couldn't write about it as she had over fifty years ago. 'We don't have to invent gods or dream of future utopias,' she said, 'for we have our own magic and creation in ourselves. Nobody really understands what life is but the fact is that the most exciting and wondrous thing we know is that we can make it, that we reproduce ourselves. And that's what young people should be taught about, the miracle of the creativity of life' (1982).

'You won't solve the riddle of the meaning of life by gazing at the stars, or building bigger and better machines,' she said, 'for the meaning of life is life itself' and Dora Russell drew my attention to some of the passages in *The Right to be Happy* where she had tried to explain this. 'Teach men and women that life is creation, that thought and imagination are creation,' she had written, and 'that each life is only valuable in so far as it uses and uses to the full every creative activity which it possesses' (p. 290). Men have looked for complexity to explain the universe, she said, when the answer is so simple and lies so close at hand.

It is this simple answer which lies so close to hand and yet which men do not see, that Dora Russell declares with great passion, *is* known to women. In our society it is women who perform the tasks which keep them in touch with the natural world, who give birth, and nurture and rear the young, who maintain the social relationships and preserve the family peace and the family ties. 'Men do not value these tasks,' she says, 'but we cannot afford their value system. We cannot accept their word, their consciousness and try to gain their approval by emulating their anti-human ways. Too many women already see the solution in male terms. Perhaps advanced industrial society has already lost so much contact with the value of life that it will cease to reproduce itself – if it does not first destroy itself with nuclear war, or pollution' (1982).

This is no simple argument that all women should have children or even that 'women and nature' share the devalued relationship which men have assigned them. There may be a biological basis for women's nurturing and caring ability or there may be no such biological basis. What we have to face is that we *don't* know and that in the long run it doesn't really matter, for this is just a red-herring which distracts our attention from what we *do* know. We know that women *are* the nurturers in our society – be it because they were so inclined or the task was forced upon them – and that not only are they skilful, but that they understand the necessity and the value of nurturing, caring, tending, conserving, mending and patching in human existence. And far from being dismissed and despised these characteristics associated with women are to be valued.

'We don't want women to stop acting like women,' said Dora Russell, 'what we want is the reverse. We can't afford any more people with anti-life values. It's men who have to stop acting like men and start acting like women' (1982).

In Dora Russell's opinion men have got to give up their commitment to the intellect, to 'pure reason' which has led them towards the creation of machines and the elevation of technology over human life: 'They have to abandon their quest for supremacy and mastery. They have to learn that they have feet of clay and are very definitely part of the physical world. They have to understand that they destroy *part of themselves* with their weapons and wars, their unchecked industrialisation and their pollution, their crazy technology and their contemptuous disregard for ecology.'

'Once,' she said, 'man used to make provision against the failure of the harvest. Now he dumps nuclear waste in the ocean and stores lethal gases' (1982).

Fundamental to Dora Russell's philosophy that machines have taken over our lives, is the understanding that these machines did not spring forth ready made. Some men invented them. Such machines are the products of male consciousness, the outcome of a particular value system which selects one option from others as more interesting, more useful, more profitable. The question that Dora Russell has been trying to answer for sixty years is *why* western man found it necessary to make such machines. His Chinese counterpart for example was propelled by no such imperative, and we can no longer subscribe to the theory that the Western way has been the superior, advanced and *civilised* way. What Dora Russell does understand is that the habit of dividing mind and body is not a universal one and that where it has not been practised man has not made a god of the machine. Not that she advocates the wholesale adoption of Eastern philosophy or the return to a life without machines. What she wants is an examination of the technological age and its values, and this is a task which she thinks most men are unable to perform so blinded are they by faith in machines. 'They have made it a religion,' she argues, 'and no one is allowed to question the dogma. And they are so bigoted that even when they can see the waste and wickedness of what they have made, they preach that the problem will be solved by more and bigger and better machines. But it's *not* new machines we want,' she says with sadness, 'its new human beings' (1982).

It was these 'new human beings' that Dora Russell wanted to emerge from her school. For sixteen years she ran the school: Bertie was not her partner for that length of time. As he had treated Alys, so too he treated Dora. 'It was bad enough only being known as the wife of Bertrand Russell,' complains Dora, 'but it was worse being known only as the *ex*-wife, or the second wife of Bertrand Russell. Would you believe that is how some people refer to me today?' I would.

There were very many pleasant times for Dora in her relationship with Bertie. Despite the financial difficulties there were happy days when they were involved in the school (although guess who had the writing room away from the noise and the demands?). Sylvia Pankhurst stayed in one of

the buildings and wrote while her son Richard joined the
school. And then there was the house in Cornwall where Dora
also had her writing hut away from the house. While it was
possible to be a father and to write in the house when the
children were around (Bertie was *not* to be disturbed) it
wasn't possible to be a mother and to write without inter-
ruption, so during the summer Dora used to make off to her
hut with her sandwiches – and her pipe – and sit at her
typewriter until Bertie, with the children, joined her in the
afternoon on the beach.

There were visitors to Cornwall, there was lively discussion and debate, and although no doubt they were mainly
Bertrand's friends, and the conversation was of his choosing
(and no doubt Dora worked twice as hard as he did), she
remembers the time with pleasure. It has not been spoiled by
the bitterness of the divorce, the deprivation of her two eldest
children, and the terrible struggle of trying to support herself
and her family. With the exit of Bertie many doors were
closed to her and it could well be that for many years she was
'blacklisted': she was certainly ignored.

Disgusted by World War I she was shocked and outraged
by World War II and intensified her efforts to promote peace
and international understanding. Her Women's Caravan of
Peace was one such effort and had much in common with
women's peace initiatives today, although, sadly, most of
the women involved today probably know nothing about the
women who went behind the 'Iron Curtain' to show that
women across nations and ideologies had more to unite than
divide them. In 1982 she still retains her faith in women's
power to expose men's insanity, but she no longer thinks that
time is on our side: 'The intoxication with industrialism and
mechanism and its application to the machines of war is
rapidly bringing us to the end,' she says (1982).

She agonises over the current state of the world with all
its crises, including its economic crises. Heretic to her finger-
tips she is a staunch opponent of productivity and gave me
one of the best lectures I have ever had on economics.

'It's quite simple really,' she said to me, 'the whole
principle of industrialism is that you have to produce more
and more every year, you have to have an expanding

economy to keep going. That means you have to have bigger and better machines that every year can produce more and more. It doesn't matter that we can't use what we produce already. No one has ever asked, "Do we need this new product?", only how many can we make and how quickly. It doesn't matter in the Western world that we've got too many of everything already – too many cars, televisions, washing machines. What matters is producing more and more. What matters is productivity!

'Can you imagine the ultimate in productivity?' she asked 'There'll be no place for human beings, just a lot of machines making so many goods in the shortest space of time – goods that human beings won't make, don't want, and can't use. Meanwhile so many are reduced to financial and psychological privation,' she said, 'while productivity rolls insanely on.' I noticed later that James Bellini – economist, broadcaster and writer – shared her view.

Financial and psychological difficulties are not unknown to Dora Russell. There has been no shortage of hardship in her life. She was divorced by Bertrand Russell, had her children taken from her, and has had close friends maimed and killed. Her younger son was badly injured in a mining accident (he was a pacifist who chose to work in a mine) and her elder son has had a severe nervous breakdown. Her granddaughter committed suicide. 'We know how to put a man on the moon but the workings of the human mind are a complete mystery to us,' she said. It is impossible to mistake her meanings.

I was numbed as I listened to Dora Russell recount her life story. She has so much courage and so much grace. She has so much compassion and such generosity. She has been, and is, a feminist who has spent her life working to make our society a more humane and responsible one. There can be no greater indictment of our society than the fact that she has been minimised, mocked or ignored: like Alexandra Kollontai whom she admired so greatly, Dora Russell has not been given her due.

Chapter 4

MARY STOTT
Born 1907

In 1929 Mary Stott was one of the first 'flapper voters' (one of the first women to vote on the same terms as men) and the fact that the term was not meant to be complimentary is not wasted on her: in 1982 she completed a three year term of office as the chairperson of the Fawcett Society – the oldest society for equality between the sexes and a society which has been campaigning for women since 1866. And between 1929 and 1982 Mary Stott has been a feminist.

As I discovered to my cost, she is incredulous when she encounters the belief that the women's movement and feminism is a fairly recent invention. When working for equality has been a constant activity in her adult life – and when she has been among so many good friends – it is understandable that she should be surprised and not amused by assertions that she, her friends, their beliefs, their actions, their organisations, their movement – never existed! It is also understandable that she should feel baffled and berated by the suggestion that feminism is but a phase that some women pass through!

'I really don't know the precise time and date I became a feminist, because there were many influences at work,' she said, 'but I knew when I *was* a feminist. I knew that I was a feminist when I went to vote in 1929. I wore a red frock because I was voting Labour – red was the Labour colour at the time – and I went into the polling booth knowing it was an historic event and conscious of performing an historic act. I knew about all those women who had spent so long and sacrificed so much so that I could be there to cast my vote on the same terms as a man. Not that actually casting the vote was so exciting,' she added, 'it was a bit of an anti-climax. I thought it should have been a much more splendid and dramatic act. But it wasn't disappointing when Labour won and I realised that I had played a part along with a lot of other women.'

What puzzled Mary Waddington – as she was then – and what still puzzles her to this day, is the number of women who not only failed to become feminists but who sought actively to dissociate themselves from feminism. 'There were women in 1929 who didn't seem to attach any great significance to the fact that they were voting. They couldn't have been ignorant of that great struggle that had gone on, yet they didn't seem to identify with it. They didn't seem to understand that it had been fought for them, that they were part of a tradition and that they had something to live up to.'

And there were still women like that today: 'A lot of women seem to have a similar attitude, – "I'm not a feminist" – and it gets wearying. What's wrong with being a feminist? I'm proud to be a feminist. It's been one of the most positive things in my life. It's one of the best traditions there is. It's admirable to be a feminist and to stand up for one's sex, to fight against inequality and injustice and to work for a better society. There can't be anything more worthwhile or more rewarding. But still you hear women say "I'm not a feminist but . . . I believe in equal rights, or equal job opportunities, or something equally feminist," and you just raise your hands in amazement and wonder *why* this reluctance to accept the name feminist.'

As Mary Stott has been a journalist since the age of eighteen, and as she is a founding member of the British Women in Media group which has been concerned with pointing to the way women are misrepresented in the media and with pressuring for change (see Josephine King and Mary Stott (eds), 1977 *Is This Your Life? Images of Women in the Media*), I asked her how influential she thought the media had been in discouraging women from becoming feminists by regularly ridiculing those who did.

'Well, of course you have a point. To my knowledge there's never been a single case of bra-burning in Britain but that hasn't stopped the media from settling on it as the standard image of "women's libbers". Feminists have often been portrayed as silly and undesirable – although I think that is changing now – and perhaps some women are turned away because they don't want to identify with a bunch of such "unpleasant" or "aggressive" women,' she said; 'But that's not all of the answer!' (1982).

'There are other women who are presented as even sillier

than feminists. Feminists aren't the only women to be mis-represented by the media. What about all the women who are portrayed as mindless drudges whose only joy in life is a particular soap powder? If women really were turned away from images that showed them as stupid or ridiculous we'd have a wholesale revolt against cleanliness! There'd be just as much reluctance to be houseproud as there would to be feminist' (1982).

Acknowledging that the media certainly hasn't helped at times, Mary Stott nevertheless feels that there is some-thing more, something she cannot quite understand, behind many women's dissociation from feminism.

For her, feminism is something which has always been there and which she has never thought of resisting. There was her mother, who despite the fact that she did not expound an explicitly feminist philosophy, nonetheless lived a feminist life, having her own job as a journalist (a remark-able feat at the beginning of this century) and a considerable involvement with women's organisations. Proudly Mary Stott states that at sixteen she became a latch-key child. There was her father who encouraged and supported her human aspirations to be an autonomous person, and there was a family climate in which it was assumed that she would work and be responsible for her own life. For her own part there was a belief that she was not the stuff from which glamorous hostesses are made, and a commitment to finan-cial independence, which helped to set her on her path: and there was also Ray Strachey's book, *The Cause*, first pub-lished in 1928.

'It made such an impression on me,' said Mary Stott, 'It was the history of the women's movement and I wanted to be part of it. All those brave women who had been so clear, so firm, so purposeful. You couldn't read about them and not know that you had a purpose, a task. You could see that a lot had been done but that there was a great deal more to do. And *The Cause* was full of so many models to look to, so many women whose example you could follow. For me it was Millicent Garrett Fawcett. She just kept on and on, without faltering for sixty years. All through my life when things have been tough, when I've worked on various campaigns

and it's taken so long and we don't seem to be getting anywhere, I've said to myself, "Remember M.G.F". Knowing she
did it is a source of strength. It keeps you going. And there,'
she said tartly, 'is another feminist who defies the "conventional wisdom", who was active for sixty years; another
woman whose whole life shows that feminism isn't something you grow out of.'

Mary Stott's first job at nearly eighteen (1925) was on the
Leicester Mail and was before the publication of *The Cause*
but she had already availed herself of some of the opportunities that the women's movement had fought for (she had
been educated at a girls' grammar school) and was on her way
to leading a life that so many of her foremothers would have
endorsed and been gratified by. But if much had been
achieved there was still a long way to go before women could
work on the same terms as men.

'As, being female, I could not belong to the Typograph-
ical Association or the Association of Correctors of the Press,
I should not really have been in the readers' room at all, but I
was tolerated as a strictly temporary copyholder,' she wrote
in 1975 in her autobiography; so one young man 'read aloud
from the galley proof and I had to follow the original, often
abominably handwritten copy, and speak up if the written
and printed words did not tally. Even in those lax times there
would have been trouble if I had actually marked the proofs'
(p. 33).

But she was in the newspaper world where she wanted to
be, learning how newspapers were put together and beginning her 'training' as a reporter: the future looked open and
positive. Even her first night at the *Mail* she was sent out on a
reporting job – to cover Miss Constance Hardcastle's pupils'
concert. Her mother went with her but the first 'masterpiece
of journalism' she wrote on her own – and it went in the paper
word for word.

Then at the age of nineteen came a terrible blow and the
first threat to the end of her short career as a *real* journalist.
She was told that she would be taking over the 'Women's
Page.'

'I went back into the Reporters' Room, put my head on
the file table and cried. I was quite right to do so. At nineteen

the door to the "real" newspaper world was being closed in my face. It was an end to my hopes' (1982).

This of course raised the old argument about the women's page – an argument that Mary Stott has been involved in for many years and one that was most definitely being conducted at the time she was put on women's issues. In 1927, in an article for *Time and Tide*, Crystal Eastman had written: 'I suppose there is nothing more irritating to a feminist than the average "Woman's Page" of a newspaper, with its out-dated assumption that all women have a common trade interest in the household arts, and a common leisure interest in clothes and the doings of "high society" ' (1978, p. 96). Women's interests were as wide as the world, argued Eastman, and to assume that all they are interested in is fashion, gossip and recipes was nearly as foolish 'as to assume that all men are interested in what to plant after wheat or the latest formula for artificial manure' (ibid.).

Not much has changed since Crystal Eastman registered her complaint. Behind the Women's Page of just about every newspaper today the idea still persists – admittedly sometimes held with greater conviction than others – that women's interests are limited, specialised, insignificant – and of low status! To be associated with women's issues then as now had its penalties, one of which more often than not is low pay.

'What should we do with the "Women's Page"?' (the title of Crystal Eastman's article) is really the tip-of-the-iceberg, of the problem of how best is women's equality to be achieved, and the question was as vigorously debated in the 1920s and 1930s (see Amanda Spry, forthcoming) as it is today. At various times it has been argued that equality will be achieved when women take their place in the public world in the same numbers as men, particularly at the policy and decision-making levels, so women will be half the politicians, the doctors, lawyers, engineers, the business executives and the bureaucrats. This would mean that the two sexes were no longer segregated with special interests of different status – you wouldn't need a Women's Page – perhaps?

The other side of this argument is that the work that women currently do *would still have to be done*, and if women were represented in the public world in the same numbers as men, then equality would demand that men be represented in the private world in the same numbers as women: but men then would be in just as much need of a Women's Page that provided household hints and quick and nutritious recipes! Indeed, on the basis of this argument half the paper might be devoted to the concerns of the public realm (from finance to football?) and half to the concerns of the private realm (from food to emotional management?).

But all of these 're-arrangements' would be, broadly speaking, within the framework of the existing social organisation: many feminists have argued that this sort of 'equality' can be achieved without any fundamental changes in society occurring, and that it isn't the sort of equality they want. Like Dora Russell they have argued that men have shaped the existing society and they don't like the shape: for them equality consists of an equal opportunity to shape society in accordance with their own different values as women. To them, the Women's Page and the values that are associated with it, are the product of male organisation: if women were in charge of society, half the time, then you wouldn't have newspapers which were almost exclusively devoted to men's interests and in which a separate, specialised, and low status space was assigned to women.

While it is absolutely necessary that there should be such debates, that women should seriously ask what equality means and how it can be achieved, we still live in an unequal world, and have to make decisions about what to do with the Women's Page. Although it may be a 'ghetto' it still seems preferable to have a space reserved for women's interests. The alternative – in an unequal society – is likely to be a newspaper in which women and women's interests are completely invisible, and *not* a newspaper which reflects the values of both sexes. And besides, while there is a Women's Page there is always the chance that it might be used to address women's 'wide-as-the-world' interests and to break away from the mould of recipes and fashion. Mary Stott may have been terribly disappointed that she was restricted to reporting on what men have decreed to be women's interests, but whenever she has had influence she has challenged that male decree, defied the limitations, and invested women's concerns with new weight and value.

'Of course this lands you right in the middle of the debate about who newspapers are for, whether they are for advertisers or readers,' said Mary Stott who has always been concerned with the philosophy behind the press. 'We get our newspapers much too cheaply, the price paid for them is less than the cost of producing them and so newspapers *must* have advertisements if they are going to survive. This means there can be a lot of pressure to run articles which will attract consumer advertising – some women's magazines for example, seem to exist mainly for the purpose of creating the peg for ads' (1982).

This 'advertising' syndrome could be the outline of a vicious circle where, without reference to women it has been decreed that women are interested in recipes and fashion: on this assumption manufacturers produce the appropriate goods: when they need to advertise them they require articles on recipes and fashion: and so the assumption that women are interested in recipes and fashion continues unchallenged . . . without any reference to women!

But this is only part of the story according to Mary Stott who had the privilege of seeing what the Women's Page of the *Manchester Guardian* was like when Vera Brittain and Winifred Holtby were writing for it earlier this century: and Mary Stott has aimed in her own work to reach the high standard such women set. 'I always believed that women were interested in more than recipes and fashion and I still think they are. But when I went as editor of the Women's Page of the *Guardian* in 1957, one colleague did jokingly accuse me of being the only Women's Page editor who wasn't interested in fashion. I was more interested in women of character than women of fashion. I really got a jolt when about 1970 we ran a questionnaire and found that many of the readers who replied wanted *more* fashion' (1982).

So fashion women get on the Women's Pages of most newspapers because it seems that they want it, and the advertisers like it. But wherever Mary Stott has been editor they have got much more besides. At nineteen, made to take over the Women's Page of the *Leicester Mail* and denied access to the training needed by a regular reporter, Mary Stott was distressed. 'I raged over being expected to have a knowledge of the domestic arts and fashion, in which I was not at all interested,' she wrote in her autobiography, 'and as a compensation for doing women's stuff, I was allowed to do theatre. "Jacques" I called myself, and thought I was pretty good. Like almost every journalist you could name, my ambition then was to be a top line theatre critic' (1975, p. 36).

And like so many women writers she chose a male pseudonym: the male has greater authority and prestige, whether it is associated with the parts of the newspaper concerned with his interests, or the articles signed by his sex. 'Jacqueline' would not have been nearly as impressive. (Later, Mary Stott – or Mary Waddington as she was then – always used her initials and wrote as 'C. M. Waddington' or 'C. M. W.' so as not to be identified as female.) The advantage of 'passing' as male is something that women have known about for a long time – for they are likely to obtain a better hearing, to be rated as more substantial, authoritative and impressive if they sign their work with a male pseudonym, hence Currer Bell and George Eliot to name but two. And it's the same old problem of the intellectual double standard. How do women get to be treated as equals when they are so frequently judged on the basis of their sex and not their work?

Elizabeth Cady Stanton, that superb American feminist of the nineteenth century (who also worked for feminism for seventy years) lost her only brother in his youth and desperately tried to replace him in her father's eyes. She had deduced that the difference between girls and boys was that boys did Latin and rode horses, and so she put much energy into these arts in order to excel. But the better she did the more her father grieved, and lamented the fact that she wasn't a boy. Having surpassed the accomplishments of her dead brother and having her father decry the fact, yet again, that she was *just a girl*, she concluded at an early age that no matter what women did it would never be granted the same worth as men, for the sole and simple reason that it was women who did it! It is the status of our sex which must be changed, she declared, for without that our achievements count for nothing.

And it is the status of the female sex that lies at the root of the problem of the devaluation of the Women's Page (or for that matter at the devaluation of women's talk, women's organisations, or women's studies), or at the devaluation of articles/books written by women.[1] One would be hard put to argue that food is a less worthy or less significant topic than football – but the 'Sports Pages' suffer not from low status.

There is yet another area where women's work is not evaluated in the same way as men's and it is one Mary Stott encountered early in her career. When a society works on the belief that the proper place for men is the paid workforce and the proper place for women is in the home, then women who cannot find work in the paid labour market are not seen to be 'out of a job' in the same way as are men. In our society it is men who are perceived as the rightful paid workers, while women are brought in, and sent home, according to the current demand. *Unemployment* then becomes a peculiarly male problem and this is no less true today than it was fifty years ago.

'In 1931 things were pretty bad and the old *Leicester Mail* was in real trouble. Some of the staff had to go and I was an obvious candidate,' said Mary Stott. 'My mother had died recently so I was a clear choice for redundancy. After all, I wouldn't be out of a job! It seemed quite reasonable to the editor to expect me to stay at home and look after my father' (1982).

We talked about the parallels today and how hidden women's unemployment is – it's even difficult to obtain statistics on it. And it so frequently goes unreported.

'I'm tired of reports on *youth* unemployment that are just about *boys*,' I said, 'Every time there is a report on television or in the paper I'm told that because of unemployment it's boys who are going to become disillusioned, alienated and violent and that's why we have to do something for the young. No one ever mentions *girls*. Katherine Clarricoates and Helen Roberts are the only two people I know who have done work on girls, and who have come out saying girls are un-employed too, in as great, if not greater numbers, than boys. But you would never know from the research community, or the media, that women are unemployed, and that *it counts just as much as male unemployment!*'

'You can't argue with the fact that women have just as many needs as men,' I continued, 'that probably as many women as men are supporting families, and that it's just as depressing, demoralising and dire for women to be out of paid work as it is for men. But when it's women, it just isn't treated as important' . . . and that, we agreed, is what feminism is about!

Mary Stott wasn't unemployed for long, however. Her father didn't agree that her place was in the home, keeping house for him. He found the advertisement that took her to the *Bolton Evening News*, where she still had to do the weekly Women's Diary but where she did get some experience in general reporting as well. And in Bolton she also came face to face with the human havoc and hardship of the recession. It was partly because she was convinced that there had to be a more sane way of organising economics that she applied for a job with the Co-operative Press, publishers of the *Co-operative News* and journals. 'Its ideology fitted me like a glove,' she said, 'because it had an idealistic basis and a practical strategy and this has always appealed to me. I thought it was a perfect system for workers' ownership and control. You didn't need capital and you didn't need capitalists' (1982).

On the *Co-operative News* she was responsible for the two pages 'devoted mainly to reports of the activites of the Women's Co-operative Guild,' but she also edited the 'fortnightly (later weekly) *Woman's Outlook*, a little magazine in the small-page old *Home Chat* format, the monthly children's magazine *Our Circle*, the monthly *Co-operative Youth*, organ of the co-operative movement's youth movement (was it mainly for boys?) and the monthly *Sunshine Stories* for the tinies' (1975, p. 39). Not a small job, and not much assistance, and she was twenty-six, and well and truly in the centre of 'women's journalism'.

'I can't remember the exact time when I started to write feminist articles,' Mary Stott said, 'When I was younger I had known I *was* a feminist and I knew what the basic issues were – after all I have experienced some of them – but I didn't really think I could do anything about it. But I took up feminist issues when I was working at the *Co-operative News*. I could see that there were things to be done and that I was in a position to do some of them.'

'But I made my first feminist gesture long before that,' she added; 'I don't know exactly when it was but I hadn't been working very long when I thought "Why should I always be the one to make the tea?" and I decided I wouldn't always be the one. And that's a principle I've practised all my working life. I've never expected anyone to make my tea, and I won't have anyone expect me to make theirs. That doesn't mean you only make tea for yourself,' she hastened to inform me, 'but when you make tea for someone else, or they make it for you, it's a friendly gesture which should be appreciated – it can't be *expected* from someone who is seen as subordinate.'

'Did you have any trouble with your male colleagues?' I asked, recalling some of the bitter wrangles of my own not-too-distant-past when I had refrained from doing more than my share of tea-making, minute-taking at meetings and food-providing at social functions. 'No one was ever nasty about it,' Mary Stott replied, 'but I must admit that there were a few who didn't understand the reason for it, who thought I was just a bit eccentric and had a thing about making tea.'

There were few such problems, however, at the *Co-operative Press* – 'women's section' – where the staff was all female. Here Mary Stott learned some of her most valuable and rewarding lessons – and not just about how a newspaper was put together or about writing unpretentiously and unpedantically in a way that could readily be understood – although these were useful skills: here she was working with the campaigning women of the Women's Co-operative Guild.

'You know all about the Co-operative Women's Guild of course,' she said to me, defying disagreement, and then added, 'even if its only from the books of letters from Co-operative guild women, edited by Margaret Llewelyn Davies'[2] She went on to give a glowing account of this magnificent woman – 'the niece of Emily Davies who had founded Girton College' – and who put all her energy into the working-class women's movement. 'It just wasn't true that the women's movement was a middle-class movement and that working-class women weren't involved,' she said, 'It's not true that it was just a fight for the vote and that only bourgeois women were concerned. It went on after the vote, and working-class women were in every campaign.'

Mary Stott reminded me of how much I take for granted and how much of what I take for granted had to be fought for. 'We had to have a campaign for birth control, a campaign for a minimum wage for women, a campaign to end the marriage bar – so women could continue to work after they were married – a campaign for women police officers, a campaign for equal divorce laws, and custody, and property settlements. The list goes on and on – and it's still going on and on, despite the Sex Discrimination Act,' she declared heatedly, and sometimes you young women forget that. But it's a tragedy if you think it all started with you, and you don't see yourselves as part of that tradition of women – working-class women among them – who campaigned for the rights you *do* enjoy today. And those women of the Guild were marvellous campaigners,' she added.

I had read the collections of letters edited by Margaret Llewelyn Davies so I did know that *Maternity* published in 1915 and which consisted of letters from Guild women describing their often horrific experiences of maternity had done a great deal to raise public consciousness about the dangers – and the despair – that were part of enforced maternity, and that the book had helped to pave the way for the birth control movement.

'The birth control movement wasn't easy,' said Mary Stott, 'it was very much like the abortion movement today – and by the way, the Guild came out very early in favour of women's equal rights in divorce – and there was a great deal of pressure on the women to abandon the campaign. At one stage the Co-operative Wholesale Society, the financial body, the *men* that handed out all the money to the various bodies, threatened to withdraw the grant it made to the Guild if they didn't stop their campaign for reforming the divorce law. It was a sizeable amount and they probably could not have continued without it, but they wouldn't give up the campaign,' she said.

They wouldn't give up either when it came to birth control; when birth control clinics were started and when coach loads of women were 'imported' to protest, on religious grounds, about birth control as murder, they remained firm. As Mary Stott described the birth control campaign of the thirties I realised that it could just as easily have been a description of the abortion campaign of the eighties. No doubt next century, (if Dora Russell's fears don't come true), women will be fighting yet another battle over reproduction and control over their own bodies. Although with the technological inventions that seem possible – and which are primarily in male hands – future issues might well be very different.

But in the 1930s Mary Stott acknowledged that along with the campaigning Guild women she was doing her bit in the *Woman's Outlook*. She wrote a series of articles on campaigning foremothers, pioneers who had worked for women's interests – Florence Nightingale, Sophia Jex Blake – and Kitty Wilkinson who started public wash-houses in Liverpool! In her editor's letter she used to suggest that just because men declared something to be wrong, women didn't have to agree with them: women were perfectly capable of making up their own minds, setting their own standards – particularly on issues that were of prime concern to women.

'You have to remember,' she said, 'that while they certainly didn't lack guts a lot of the women lacked confidence. They'd often only had a bare minimum of schooling and were used to being faced with authority, not with *being* authorities themselves. And this is where the Guild helped to give them so much confidence and faith in their own judgment. There was a marvellous sense of solidarity. And there was new strength and assurance when so many of them found that they felt the same way and agreed with each other,' she said.

But it was also the training which the Guild provided for its members which helped to promote purpose and self-esteem. Mary Stott is the first to recognise that today its rigid hierarchical structure looks silly, restrictive, and unnecessary, but this does not take away the value of the contribution that the Guild made to so many women's lives. With its firmly defined rules and methods of procedure it provided a clear framework in which women were secure, and where they could move step by step through the various stages, gaining in self-assurance and stature all the time. 'It was training, knowledge, education, that the women would not otherwise have had,' she maintained; 'so many of them, so young, had been confined to kitchens, (their own and those of employers), to very long hours of work, and there was a lot of pressure on them to stay there. And the Guild and its meetings and activities opened up new horizons for them, and a new way of life. It was a social occasion but much more as well. There was the indirect training provided by the meetings, but there were also specialist classes; classes for speaking in public, classes on meeting procedure, classes on specialist subjects. Sometimes the classes were held in different places at weekends and the women went off and left their families to go to training schools run by the Guilds. Arguments about domestic responsibilities and the duties of a good wife and mother aren't new ones,' she added with a smile – and a sigh, 'Those women were truly heroic!' (1982).

Mary Stott well understands the reasoning behind the non-hierarchical and more open structural arrangements of the modern women's movement and she respects and endorses those reasons. Yet although she would never want to return to some of the restrictions that characterised the structures of the women's organisations which emerged after the vote was won, she believes that to some extent today's feminists *have* 'thrown the baby out with the bathwater'.

'It may not be so difficult if you have confidence to begin with,' she said, 'because you can step in and get on with it. But if you are unsure of yourself and what to do, there aren't any guidelines to help you. And you can go on feeling more and more inadequate when other women seem to be able to handle it all, and you can't. It doesn't help when you can't see how it is done, when there are no stages or graded tasks that can help to ease you into playing your part.'

Mary Stott was referring to 'public' meetings and helped to show that there has been a real swing of the pendulum over the last fifty years because many contemporary feminists may not even have had experience of such 'public' meetings, which is probably one of the reasons there has been no great need to evolve more formal structures. Today's 'groups' are significantly smaller than were the national organisations associated with the suffrage movement and the citizenship movements which followed. Most contemporary 'groups' are formed around friendships, or shared interests, or a particular campaign.

The consciousness raising groups which sprang up in the late sixties and the seventies – and which were the nucleus of the present movement – were small groups which had the specific aim of exploring the *personal* and making connections. They too allowed women to gain confidence and to understand that they felt the same about many issues. They too allowed communication among women and directly and indirectly led to new horizons and a new way of life. Women in consciousness raising groups got to know each other intimately, and didn't have the need of formalised structures – partly because people who know each other so well find that the structure is provided by personal knowledge. In small, personal groups, it is possible for every member to appreciate the various needs of other members and to provide support, encouragement and space, and in these circumstances guidelines or rules about procedures, responsibilities or tasks can be quite superfluous.

When we talked about past and present structures I couldn't pretend, of course, that all *does* operate perfectly today, and that the open-ended nature of many women's meetings (particularly if they are *not* small and the members do *not* know each other well) is the best possible form of organisation under all circumstances. I was very ready to acknowledge that we might have something to learn from the way women have organised in the past. But I wasn't ready to acknowledge that formal structures were always the best form of organisation either. 'It's not black and white, you know,' I said, 'because I've been to a few big public meetings which have been conducted along formal lines and it hasn't exactly boosted my confidence to know that there are rules, and correct ways of doing things. On the contrary I have been intimidated. I'm sure there has to be a blend of the two. I just can't cope when I'm informed that the meeting is being conducted according to "Roberts Rules of Parliamentary Procedure" or whatever.'

And I couldn't resist telling Mary Stott about my theory: why it is that men have found it necessary to devise such complicated rules for talking to each other? 'It's because they all talk and interrupt so much, and they're all so concerned with "having the floor" that they have had to work out the strictest and most rigid rules just to have some order. Women don't need such rules,' I added semi-facetiously, but with reference to recent research which suggests that men define 'successful conversation' as having *their* say, and women define it as everyone having a fair turn (see Elizabeth Aries, 1976).

In a more serious vein we talked of possible alternative arrangements. 'One of the best examples I know of was in Canada,' I said, and went on to tell Mary Stott about a national conference that was held where so many women came from so many parts of the country – and didn't know each other. 'They had to have some rules but they wanted them to be negotiable and they didn't want any autocratic rulings with people "out of order". So one of the first things they did was to have a "feminist chair" – three women were the "chairperson". When there were any problems the three women discussed them – with the microphone on – and came to an agreement. Everybody at the meeting knew why certain decisions were being made. And of course it had the added advantage that no *one* woman was put under pressure and later "blamed" for making the wrong decision. I'm sure if we thought more about it we could come up with some innovative ways of running big "public" meetings in satisfactory ways,' I added, 'but too often at the moment it's dogma and not pragmatics that prevails. You didn't need chairpersons, procedural guidelines and minutes-secretaries in the old consciousness raising groups but you need something as a realistic base for running big meetings and national conferences.'

Then we found ourselves in the middle of an animated discussion. To Mary Stott, many of the big, 'public' and structured women's organisations were 'a thing of the past' and I realised for the first time that to me, the smaller, private, and personally structured women's organisations of consciousness raising groups were also in many respects 'a thing of the past'. I don't *go* to any CR groups anymore.

This may be nothing other than a personal dimension. There were times – almost a decade ago now – when for me, the weekly consciousness raising (CR) session was the high point of the week. It was where a whole new world was unfolding and I can remember the intensity of the experience – both the pleasure and the pain. But I can also see why CR groups were so vital at that stage . . . for after all, they were really the *only* source of information we had for making sense of our lives. Sometimes it is difficult to remember what it was like when there were only a handful of feminist books (and it is even more difficult to explain to those who have grown up in an age of feminist publishers and publications); but there were only a few books and we had all read them; they were a basis of shared experience and we built on those books in CR sessions. But perhaps with the advent of feminist publishers – and women's studies courses, and women's groups in and out of the work place – CR sessions are not required to play the crucial role they once did. Besides, these days it is so much more acceptable and so much more common for women to meet together, and engage in consciousness raising, that the need for setting aside a special time in the week is not so pressing.

In the presence of Mary Stott it was pleasant to reflect upon the changes within the women's movement – even over the last decade. I found myself patterning my own past (and re-evaluating it, and being prepared to reconsider and to change) as I listened to her patterning the women's movement of the twentieth century. Seen through her eyes, in an historical context and with the added dimension of her own practical experience in many facets of the women's movement – old and new – it all became more concrete and more meaningful.

Currently, one can see how CR groups have evolved into a variety of women's ventures; many women now are working around particular issues where a great deal of consciousness raising goes on – the Greenham Common Peace Movement, Women Against Violence Against Women, the

300 Group (which aims to get three hundred women into parliament), PROS (Programme for Reform of the Law on Soliciting), Wages for Housework, Women in Media – and many, many more: and women have organised around different projects – Lesbian Line, the Women's Research and Resources Centre, Women's publishing, women's newsletters and information, not to mention women's committees in trades unions, on councils and in many other areas of 'public' life. But there is now no 'umbrella organisation' which can speak with a public voice and exert considerable pressure on behalf of a multitude of women with diverse interests but a common cause.

It's possible to argue that the current feminist groups, are grass roots groups, small and autonomous and linked to each other by a network – I frequently do argue this way! But listening to Mary Stott, respecting her wisdom and her wealth of experience which spans the old and the new, I had the sneaking suspicion that it was possible to argue that the women's movement today is somewhat fragmented and lacks the force and the public voice that a national umbrella association has provided in the past.

Contemporary feminists know full well the extent to which the division of public and private – so central to a male dominated society and so convenient for men – has worked against women. Are we becoming its victims once again? Are we at the moment caught in its web of limitations and will future generations 'pass judgment' on us for our short sightedness about the power of the private in the way that (too) many of us have 'passed judgment' on our foremothers for their short sightedness about the power of the public.

Earlier this century the women's movement was *public*. The rationale behind militancy was *not* to win a battle based on force, but to make public the contempt in which women were held, and to demonstrate that far from practising the chivalry they professed towards the fair sex, many men revealed that they were prepared to engage in systematised violence against women – in the open – and that they valued their material property more than they valued women.

The public women's movement *was* political pressure, from disrupting men's meetings to lobbying: it was a

National Union of Societies for Women's Suffrage: it was public figures, public meetings and public voices.

But from the outset the current women's movement went *private*. It is understandable that it should have taken this course. After all the public women's movement hadn't exactly achieved liberation for most women for whom much of their oppression was located in the private domain of 'the home'. It was because this vast area of women's structured subordination was as entrenched as it had ever been that women recognised that the so-called private and *personal was political* and began to argue that politics begins at home. And consciousness raising groups were conducted primarily within private homes – one reason being that there was little or no public space for women to meet (no equivalents to working men's clubs, or sporting clubs, or pubs for women), and another reason being that the home was in many cases the 'battle ground'.

There had to be this emphasis on relationships, on attitudes, on consciousness. There was no public or legal way of confronting the problem of women's service for men: 'You couldn't have a national conference and pass a resolution that henceforth men will be responsible for their own shit-work – even if it was procedurally in order and reported widely and fairly in the public press,' I said, 'and then realistically expect that men would take notice and change the habits of a lifetime. It was absolutely essential that women start with the problems in the home.'

'I couldn't agree more,' Mary Stott replied, 'but just as not everything will be solved in public, nor will everything be solved in private. Don't you think we need both?' (1982). And I found that I couldn't agree more – which put a very different slant on our discussion of the women's movement.

For me, there was a real puzzle. I had found myself unintentionally acknowledging that I thought consciousness raising groups were no longer the heart of the women's movement. Obviously, it wasn't because the problem had been solved and that men were now doing their full share of the housework, child care and family maintenance. I was too aware of the growing body of research which suggests that in most cases the idea of 'equal partnership' is little more than a

myth and that a man can be seen as *sharing* domestic responsibilities when he *helps* a woman with the shopping, does the
dishes *for her*, or *babysits*. Women are neither praised nor
thanked in general for helping a man with the shopping,
doing the dishes for him, or babysitting!

'Helping' may be progress when judged against a background of men declaring that all domestic work is women's
work and men are demeaned by it – but it certainly isn't
equality. And not even all men go so far as to 'help'. So if the
solution hadn't been found, why did consciousness raising
groups cease to be so central? Have they really been replaced
by more effective forms of organisation?

And perhaps more importantly, what is the structure
and purpose of the *existing* movement? These were not easy
questions (and in terms of my own politics they were ones I
would prefer not to dwell upon) but as Mary Stott talked of
her past and present experience in the women's movement I
found myself entertaining possibilities I had not thought of
before. True the discussion was challenging (at times I think
it was downright threatening for me) but I began to understand just how much we have been denied by not knowing our
past: I began to appreciate just what raw novices we can be
when instead of drawing on and building on the insights of
our foremothers, we start from scratch.

'I am an organisation woman,' Mary Stott stated firmly,
'because I think the only way women are going to get anywhere is by organising. And I mean *all* forms of organising.
You can't dismiss any women's organisation.' She knows
much about women's organisations: she has worked in some
(the Women's Co-operative Guild), been members of some
(Women in Media, The Fawcett Society) and has studied
some. In 1978 she published *Organization Women: The Story
of the National Union of Townswomen's Guilds* in which she
traced the origin, purpose – and success – of these guilds
which came to have more than a quarter of a million
members.

'I wrote the book partly because I'm interested in organisation, and so little is known about the way women have
organised. It's virtually invisible,' she said. 'I wrote it partly
because I wanted women to know what excellent things

women have been doing for themselves and others during this century. And,' she added with force, 'I wrote it partly because I was sick of hearing that women couldn't work together.'

'Women, in fact, have banded together for all sorts of reasons, as they still do. They have banded together for political purposes: to fight oppressive laws and economic conditions; to raise the status of women from that of criminals, bankrupts and minors; to succour the deprived; to achieve improvements in the education, health and welfare of women and children; to give one another support in their trades and professions; to widen their own horizons; to have an escape from the confining four walls of home. And they have banded together for company and friendship, because contrary to a powerful old myth,' (and it isn't difficult to detect the origin of it; Mary Stott suggests it is a self-protective male invention) 'they *like* being together' (1978, p. 1).

This was true of the Townswomen's Guilds: women liked being together, and together they accomplished some marvellous things.

While the Townswomen's Guilds created a centre for women and women's activities, and while many women who joined became increasingly concerned with women's rights, unlike the Six Point Group, or the Fawcett Society, the guilds were not directly concerned with campaigns for women's equality.

'You mustn't be frightened of reevaluating your position, taking stock and changing direction,' Mary Stott said, 'for lots of women have done it before. It's what women had to do when the vote looked like becoming a reality. There were societies – and funds – and all these trained women who could see that they were in sight of achieving the goal of the vote. But they also knew that the vote was a beginning, not an ending, and they set about redefining their goals and rechannelling their efforts to meet new demands. The National Union of Women's Suffrage Societies became the National Union of the Societies for Equal Citizenship and at the annual council meeting in March, 1927 they decided that "This Council resolves itself into a committee to consider by what means those about-to-be-franchised women who do not yet belong to the women's movement may be drawn into active co-operation with it." And with that in mind it was some of the women who were on that committee who went out and started the Townswomen's Guilds' (1982).

How did Mary Stott know all this? Partly because she made it her business to find out and because she had gone to talk to some of the women who were involved. *Organization Women* makes use of the reminiscences of Margery Corbett Ashby who in her ninety-fifth year explained to Mary Stott how the guilds had come into being. We *can* construct women's continuity even when it is not automatically handed to us and made the substance of our education.·

The women who started the guilds did want to involve women who hadn't previously been associated with the women's movement so they certainly wanted to make the Townswomen's Guilds 'attractive'. They wanted to provide a space for women to meet each other, to exchange experiences and skills, to hear visiting speakers, to become more confident, have wider interests – and to make good use of their vote. In the words of Margery Corbett Ashby they wanted to make possible comradeship, citizenship training, and the development of crafts and interests. So in the old suffrage headquarters in Dean's Yard, with £100 from the MP Eleanor Rathbone and considerable determination, some of the old suffrage workers re-evaluated their role, redefined their priorities and purpose, and the Townswomen's Guilds were launched.

There were twenty-six guilds within a year: 'The pioneers said they planned carefully,' wrote Mary Stott, 'developing solidly, not fast, and that they spent a lot of time working out programmes which would be most suitable for different types of guild, but twenty-six guilds in a year was an astonishing achievement, and . . . they had the confidence to rent an office and staff.' Such success did not magically materialise, however, but was the result of 'grinding organizational effort' with women who were already up to their ears in work still finding time 'to go knocking on the doors of women whose names had been given to them by the old regional suffrage organisers to invite people to introductory meetings. Often only five or six turned up and it might take

two or three meetings before sufficient women showed
interest to make forming a guild worthwhile' (1978, p. 11).

'A campaign for recruits! Is that what we need today?' I
asked and began to speculate on the possibilities. We have so
many diverse and excellent women's studies programmes
that we could go from door to door and invite women to come
along. Would it be so very different from what the pioneers
did for the guilds? We would probably have to add some joy
and celebration to some of the women's studies programmes –
it has always been a grievance of mine that so much knowledge women have generated is so depressing: it is unde-
niable that much of what we know is depressing but much is
also joyous and also deserves a place. How about hand-outs –
'Come and join the feminists and improve your quality of life'
or 'Join the women's movement and improve your IQ' – for
there is such an explosion of knowledge and understanding
when one becomes a feminist that it is sure to be reflected in
IQ tests!

Could we – in no time – have a National Union of
Societies for Women's Liberation with hundreds of branches
across the country meeting regularly; could we have a central
office and staff, an annual national conference – and an influx
of new members who in the words of that 1927 resolution
have not yet been drawn into active co-operation in the
women's movement?

And would we then be in a better and stronger position to
fight the public issues of women's employment and unemployment, of low pay and discrimination, of sexual harassment and violence: would we be in a stronger position to
argue for an end to racism, for peace and conservation, for
more sane ways of organising the world? It is a question
which bears thinking about.

For Mary Stott the struggle has always been one conducted primarily in public. She was fortunate enough to be
married to a man with whom she did have an exceptionally
egalitarian relationship: they were both journalists and for
much of their life together she worked during the day and he
worked at night. It was a remarkably liberated relationship:
Mary Stott did not take too kindly to those who expressed
regret and sympathy at the arrangement whereby two adults

led full, independent and yet co-operative lives. But it still has to be admitted that not all women live with men who happily do the vegetables and willingly assume domestic responsibilities – that so few similarly inclined men are to be found is the reason that many women give for *not* living with men. Not all women find themselves emotionally supported by men and indeed, many women find themselves physically and psychologically attacked while the politics of dominance prevails: and not all women have interesting and rewarding paid work which allows them satisfaction and financial independence. Mary Stott knows this: it is one of the reasons she has put so much energy into campaigning for women's equality.

Besides, while there have been some areas where she has not directly experienced the full force of patriarchy, there are other areas where the message that she is a woman in a male dominated society have been delivered loud and clear. Not allowed to join the union or correct proofs when she commenced work, denied a place in mainstream journalism, made redundant because she could take on the job of looking after her father – these were not the least of the discriminatory blows delivered in her working life. During the war she took over more and more responsibility for the *Co-operative News* and then in 1942 the editor left to take over *Reynolds News*: 'the only obvious candidate (for the editorship of the *Co-operative News*) who was available was me,' she wrote 'and I was female' (1975, p. 42).

She didn't get the job and was later informed, 'There's no doubt you would have got it if you had worn trousers.' The objection to Mary Stott as editor was that it would be a bit awkward as she had to deal with so many *men* from the Co-operative Wholesale Society and the Co-operative Union.

And then in 1945 she applied for a job as a news sub-editor on the *Manchester Evening News*: the good news is that she got the job – when it was thought, and still is thought by many men, that women are incapable of being sub-editors. The bad news is that after a few weeks on the duty rota as a 'copy-taster' (the person who sifts the incoming copy, handing out the lesser items to sub-editors and passing on major items to the chief sub-editor) her name was dropped from the duty rota.

' "Why" I asked the chief sub. "Don't I measure up?" "It was the editor's decision," he said. So . . . I went to the editor, Tom Henry. Tom was honest and explicit. "We have to safe-guard the succession, Mary, and the successor has to be a man." So I had to go.' (1977, p. 47).

'It's one of the reasons I feel so passionately about equal employment opportunity and why I will fight and fight; she said, 'so that no one can say you can't do something because you are a woman. If my grand-daughters want to be plumbers or conduct an orchestra I want them to be able to do so without anyone trying to stop them simply because they are female' (1982).

It might be a long time however before women are sub-editors: Women in Media conducted a questionnaire about women's employment and one editor replied with: 'Subbing is not suitable for women. The pace is too hectic.'

'Well, it makes a change from toilets,' I said; 'At least he didn't write "Women cannot be sub-editors because we have no toilets for them." '

The Women in Media group has been for Mary Stott a major focus for the fight for women's equality. Founded in 1970 by a small group of women journalists, including Mary Stott, the group quickly expanded to include women from radio, television, magazines, publishing, advertising, the theatre, cinema, and public relations. 'Concerned that so much of our culture trivializes and exploits women we wanted to break down discrimination by examining the con-ditions of women's work and promotion opportunities, and to provide facts to influence change. We had no rules and there was no membership qualification. Any woman concerned to help free women from the limitations imposed on them by society in work, at home, in public or in private life was welcome,' she wrote with Josephine King in 1977 in their Introduction to a selection of articles on women in the media.

'Many members knew what it was like, personally or through friends and colleagues, to be told either bluntly or by implication: "You can't do that. You're a woman." Many worked at the BBC where until recently it was almost Holy

Writ that women couldn't read the news, much less be *seen* to read it' (1977, p. 1).

While I don't want to put a dampener on the achievements of Women in Media – which have been considerable – I still think it is important to point out that 'progress' isn't as simple as it seems. There was a time when the BBC *did* think women were suitable news readers – during the war when it was thought desirable for the men to hear a woman's voice! Those women disappeared very quickly when the war was over, and the BBC quickly reverted to its policy of declaring that women's voices weren't suitable for the serious business of reporting the news – and sporting results.

And even today, while there are *more* women news-readers on the radio (although they are by no means *half*) it has to be noted that radio is the poor relation and that the pattern of women's employment has generally been to 'let women in' after power and prestige have left. (My sister, Lynne Spender fervently declares that one of the reasons women have been 'let into' publishing in increased numbers of late is because the printed word is becoming the poor relation with the explosion in 'high tech' information: in Britain there are now more video shops than book shops: see Lynne Spender, 1983.)

Sadly, when it comes to women's issues there is no such thing as winning a battle once and for all: too frequently some women are let into particular positions in response to a demand, but when the demand ceases, so too do the appointments. We find that there is a drift back to males being considered the most suitable candidates. No doubt if Women in Media conducted a survey at the BBC today there would be many who would vehemently declare that there was *no* discrimination against women, who would be prepared to argue that there were as many women news-readers as men – and who would even go so far as to insist that it was just the other way around, and that it was men who were likely to be discriminated against because outright favouritism was being shown to women! The name given to this form of behaviour is called *backlash*: it means protesting that things have gone far enough *before* inroads are made into your power base. Such is the effect of a few women *main* newsreaders for a relatively short period of time.

Women in Media raised these issues and was active on many fronts. Many of the members worked on newspapers 'where the executive jobs almost without exception, are held by men, and where the assumption is maintained, as in women's magazines, that men know best what women want,' and in the face of this, Women in Media found itself almost inevitably drawn into the public forum, acting as a campaigning pressure group to fight discrimination. Because 'of the knowledge many of us have of the way the media operate,' wrote Josephine King and Mary Stott, 'because of specialist skills and opportunities to write and broadcast, we were soon in the front line of women's groups, which were mobilizing fast to put pressure on Parliament and the civil service to make radical changes on behalf of women. Fleet Street began to modify its mocking attitude to the women's movement, and the BBC was forced to look at the blatant discrimination against women within its organisation' (1977, p. 2).

'I cannot understand how other women cannot see the changes that I think are necessary,' said Mary Stott, 'I cannot understand why they cannot see the marvellous things about feminism, about what it's fighting for and what friendships, what fun and joy there can be within it. For me, there are so many unforgettable memories – that night in 1973 when Women in Media had a torchlight procession from parliament to Downing Street. I walked between Mikki Doyle, women's editor of the *Morning Star*, and Una Kroll, who was a doctor and a deaconess of the Church of England. And next day in the newspapers there were photographs of women's faces lit up by the flares, and they were beautiful, happy, joyous faces. Why is it that there are women who simply cannot appreciate what women's liberation is all about?' (1982).

Women in Media has not been the only women's organisation in which Mary Stott has been involved in the last few years and in which she has found such friendship, support, and purpose. She has been a member – and chairperson – for the Fawcett Society, for which she wrote the pamphlet 'The

Long March to Equality: a short history of the Fawcett Society' (1982).

'It's been going for over one hundred years – although it hasn't always had the same name,' she told me. 'And it's been a single-minded fight to do away with all sex discrimination – "Whether based in law, practice or custom". It was started in 1866 when a handful of women in the space of two weeks got more than fifteen hundred signatures for a petition for women's suffrage, which John Stuart Mill was to present in parliament. And the women who are in the Fawcett Society today are no less dedicated or determined than those women were then.'

'Of course they knew the vote wouldn't solve women's problems, no more than the Sex Discrimination Act or the Equal Pay Act or the existence of the Equal Opportunities Commission will bring an instant end to discrimination "in law, practice or custom". But they do make a difference,' insisted Mary Stott, 'because it actually makes it *illegal* to discriminate against women. Changes in attitude, and habit, can follow changes in the law. And we have had a century of stage-by-stage improvements in the law and improvements in women's position. You just can't ignore the women teachers and civil servants who went on nagging and nagging for equal pay and an end to the marriage bar. If, like me, you had had to go to your employer to see if you were *allowed* to stay on at work after you were married, you'd have much more idea about how it feels to be so deeply enmeshed in laws that discriminated *against* you. It's even a mammoth achievement that discrimination has virtually gone from the laws themselves,' she said firmly (1982).

'You just *can't* hold the view that there hasn't been any progress,' she said, 'because it denies all those years of struggle and those great achievements. Of course we still have a long way to go, but we have come a long way too, in one hundred years. And if you don't accept that then all those women count for nothing!' (1982).

I am used to women 'counting for nothing' in a patriarchal society: I am not used to thinking that I make a contribution to the process. Yet each time I dismiss the efforts of women past – or present – that have been designed to improve women's position in society I add to the erasure of women from our cultural heritage.

Through Mary Stott – and the librarians of the Fawcett Library – I have come to know a great deal about the Fawcett Society and I have come to be proud of its long record of campaigns for women's rights. I have become a member and have found in the Fawcett Society many of the features that Mary Stott has outlined – friends, fun, a philosophy I can readily understand and numerous projects devoted to women's interests in which I can participate. And I can see why it serves patriarchal ends to make disparaging or dismissive comments about women's efforts to attain equality.

I have come to appreciate that accusations of 'bourgeois' and 'reactionary' which have been levelled against so many women from Barbara Bodichon to Christabel Pankhurst (and which cannot be substantiated) are nothing other than 'name-calling', the propaganda of a patriarchal society. Just as this technique has been used to discredit women of the past, to divide us from them and break our continuity, so too can it be used to discredit women of the present and to divide us from each other.

While I am aware of the devaluation of women as it is practised today and I am always on my guard lest I be taken in, it seems I am not nearly so careful when it comes to the devaluation of women in my immediate past. I would never just accept an educational report, for example, which states that women underachieve, or a psychological report that claims that women are unstable – without asking *who* is responsible for such 'findings' and what do they have to gain by them? Yet it seems I have too readily accepted derisory reports about women of the past and that I have not always applied my 'litmus test' of asking who puts forward these 'findings' and what do they have to gain – if we believe them? I have not always tried to find the reasons behind the dismissal of so many women as 'bourgeois' or 'reactionary' but instead have 'dismissed' them and in the process denied myself the opportunity of finding out about them and of placing them as positive figures in women's past.

What we have to recognise is that the more fronts women work on for liberation, the stronger we will be. We need to look again at our foremothers, as Mary Stott has suggested, and to look more closely at the way they organised, the strategies they used and the achievements they made. We need our past to make sense of our present and our future. We cannot afford to be arrogant, to assume that we are the first, or even the first to get it right! This is precisely what we are meant to think: it is how we divide ourselves from our foremothers and help to bury our own history.

The Fawcett Society is our oldest society concerned with the fight for equality. It *has* continuity. It does build on accumulated wisdom and as such is unique for women. It does try to utilise some of the foundations of the past to strengthen the present: in 1980, along with Women in Media it acted as an 'umbrella' when it organised *Women's Day of Action* and brought together seventy different women's organisations. From this day a plan of action emerged, 'Eight Points for the Eighties', a programme and priorities for the continuing campaign for women's equality.

'You have been fighting for a long time,' I said to Mary Stott – 'don't you ever get weary and even tempted to give up?'

Her response was energetic and indignant: 'Not a bit of it. There are so many things to keep us going. We do have our successes – and remember Millicent Garrett Fawcett! The fighting and campaigning I can understand, and always want to be part of – even when there are setbacks – it's withdrawal and giving up that I *can't* understnd. That's what I think so many women did during the fifties and I never could understand it. And I can't understand women today who cannot see the splendid value of feminism.'

She went on to describe some of the 'ups and downs' in her struggle for women's rights and the way she saw them in an historical context: 'I can remember sitting in the gallery of the House of Commons in 1972 when they were trying to get a second reading on the Anti-Discrimination Bill. And you couldn't be there waiting to see what the politicians would do without thinking of the Suffragettes who time and again had sat behind that grille – waiting for the outcome. There were rows of women there in 1972, watching and listening, but it was Shirley Williams who was at the despatch box. And the reason she was there was because those women of the past worked so hard. And women in the future will benefit from some of our work. When I listened to Shirley Williams and watched all those women in the gallery, I knew why I was a feminist. It is a long march to equality. Of course,' she added, 'our bill got talked out in 1972 and many of the women were bewildered and frustrated. But I knew it had happened before and it would happen again, it's part of the journey. And we *did* get our second reading. The excitement and celebration then. There was so much hugging and kissing – and that's happened before and will happen again – although I don't know if it had ever taken place in the Central Lobby before with all those happy women shouting "We've won." '

To Mary Stott, each step is a step closer to the goal: there are fewer and fewer gaps to be plugged as women make more and more gains. She is an optimist – and a realist – and her values come from a deep understanding of women's history, and an assurance of women's continuity. Perhaps if I had shared her experience of women's traditions I would also share her optimism. I must admit, however, I retain some of my reservations, despite the fact that her views had done much to challenge – and to shift – my own.

In many ways Mary Stott's life embodies the history of the women's movement this century, since the vote was won. Her involvement with women's issues spans the older and the newer forms of organisation (and she readily and eagerly made the transition from the old to the new) and in many respects she represents a blend of the best of both. She has used her strength and her skills inside and outside the paid work force in the service of women: she has done much to make public the discrimination against women and she has done much in private to make this possible – all those weary-ing and invisible organisational hours that lie behind the success of Women in Media, The Fawcett Society, and Women's Day of Action.

She has worked on committees, been a member of depu-tations, has written letters, attended meetings, made sub-missions, drafted reports, given speeches – and written regularly for the Women's Pages. For almost sixty years she has been rousing women – and men – and she is a rich source of inspiration, ideas, strategies, plans, all aimed at ending the discrimination against women.

She is a tangible link with the women's movements of earlier generations whose advice is well worth listening to.

CONSTANCE ROVER
Born 1910

When Constance Rover retired in the early seventies she was the Deputy Head of the Department of Sociology and Law at the Polytechnic of North London, and for many years she had been doing research on women. Her PhD had been on the women's suffrage movement and in 1967 she had published *Women's Suffrage and Party Politics in Britain 1866–1914*, and *The Punch Book of Women's Rights* – the latter undertaken, she explains, as a form of light relief. In 1970 she published *Love, Morals and the Feminists*, and these books, the outcome of many years of work, all had their source in an interest which predates the contemporary women's movement. Constance Rover was doing research on women at a time when we are reliably informed that women were not a topic: it was quite salutary for me to learn that while I was finding my way through my 'womanless' university education in Australia – and even reading courses in modern British History where with the exception of Queen Victoria, never a woman was mentioned, Constance Rover was in London, frequently at the Fawcett Library, reading and writing about all those wonderful women from an earlier women's movement.

I asked her if she could explain her 'untimely' interest in women's history and she replied that it was one of the few areas which allowed her to combine her major interests in law, politics, history – and women! So, of course my next question was how she came to be interested in women and to see women as a *bona fide* research area, when interest in women, in the early sixties, was supposed to be at an all time low. Again, my own assumptions were challenged: why should she *not* have been interested in women, she asked me?

Even now I find it difficult to adequately explain and accept those great gulfs that divide the generational experience of women. In the early sixties I managed to do an Arts Degree and to conclude after three years 'liberal' education that women had no past and that apart from the occasional exceptional woman – Jane Austen, George Eliot, and of course Queen Victoria (who was almost always mentioned in a derisory manner) – women had made no contribution to our culture and were therefore indisputably, and justifiably, the second sex. For me, then, the modern women's movement was the beginning of a whole new way of life, of questioning the education I had received, the habits I had acquired, the beliefs I had formed – including the belief that women were not present in the valued knowledge of society because women had nothing of value to contribute.

And I had assumed that my experience was much the same for other women – and I think perhaps it was for women of my own age. Yet while we were bubbling with excitement at what we believed to be our new found discoveries, while we presumed that we were pioneers, there were older women who had for many years understood much of what we were *re*-discovering. But there were few if any channels of communication between us.

Constance Rover was born and brought up in Cumberland, on the edge of the Lake District and has many memories of unemployment and poverty in the area. The steel works which expanded during World War I could not survive on the same scale when steel was no longer required after the war: there was the miners' strike and much hardship. Fortunate enough to finish school and to obtain potential university entrance, she was unable to go to university and became instead a legal secretary when her father died. 'I was always reading,' she said; 'I just loved reading and I dearly would have liked to go to university, but it just wasn't possible.' There was, however, the option of an external degree, which she later took – graduating at the age of thirty-eight. Then there was part-time lecturing in WEA (Workers' Educational Association) courses, and in the field of further education then full time work at the North Western Polytechnic (which later merged with the Northern Polytechnic to become the Polytechnic of North London).

'I was always twenty years too late,' she said, 'twenty years late getting my degree, twenty years late working in education.' Looking at her interests and the work she has done, it could be said that she was twenty years (almost) too early. She was the first to introduce in Britain what we would now call a 'women's studies' course: it was in the early seventies and included her own contribution – a comparison between the 'old' and the 'new' women's movements.

Constance Rover found it difficult to identify the time and place she became a feminist: 'I didn't join any women's organisations when I was young,' she said, 'partly because work and all my other commitments simply didn't leave enough time. But then when I was married and working part-time, I joined the Women's Citizens' Association. It was non-party, but it was still quite political, and very much concerned with *women's* interests. It was one of the associations formed *after* women got the vote and its objectives were to ensure that women could use the vote responsibly. It was social but it was also informative, and educative. I suppose you could say it was a structured interest in current affairs, and a consideration of how they would affect women' (1982).

There were guest speakers: 'It was where I first heard Vera Brittain speak,' Constance Rover said, indicating her early and enduring interest in women. Teresa Billington Greig (of suffragette fame), and Helena Normanton – the first woman barrister and a formidable campaigner for women's rights, were also speakers who impressed and inspired.

And after the Women's Citizens' Association, there was the Suffragette Fellowship, of which Constance Rover became a member. 'It went on for years,' she said, 'although for obvious reasons it has wound up now – there aren't too many suffragettes left to meet. But many of those women were fascinating, and such a mine of information.' And they were sometimes women on whom Constance Rover was already doing research. Right back in her WEA days she had given lectures on 'The Status of Women' and had started to cultivate her interest in women's struggle for the vote. 'I was already researching women's suffrage when I joined both the Fawcett Society and the Suffragette Fellowship,' she said.

She tried to explain what the women's movement was before the current renaissance. 'We didn't know the women's liberation movement was coming and you must try and understand what it was like. We thought we *were* the women's movement because we didn't know there could be a different *form* of women's movement. After the vote we thought our task was to fight to remove existing legal inequalities and to keep a watching brief on laws, regulations and customs that discriminated against women. Equal Pay was a big issue, and the removal of the marriage bar. And there were things like the fact that the passport practices weren't comparable – a man could have his wife on his passport, but not the other way around. And the laws about guardianship of infants favoured men. And then there was a court ruling about a woman's house-keeping money not belonging to her – all those things had to be sorted out and we put a lot of energy into getting it right so at the point that the new movement started, none of those issues were there to get in the way.'

'There are still some anomalies,' I pointed out, 'particularly in the area of nationality bills. "Citizenship" is still passed on through men and not women when children are born outside Britain. And there is the law where racism and sexism are intertwined – where black and Asian women can't bring their spouses into the country, but where men can.'

Still, there is no denying the fact that when the 'new' women's movement burst upon the scene our aspirations were not cluttered to the same extent as our foremothers' with the need to reform laws so that women who were married could own property – or obtain divorces – and at least there were no *laws* against married women working, even if there were many established practices which kept women out of various fields of employment and kept women in general in low paid and low skill jobs. (Why, I ask myself is almost the entire catering staff of British Rail, male: and why when men have structured career paths for themselves from the shop floor to the manager's office is there no such path from secretary to manager, or nurse to doctor?)

From the beginning of the feminist renaissance (as Liz Stanley calls it) the focus was on *attitudes* rather than on laws, but it does seem reasonable to assume that women were able to put the emphasis on consciousness raising because discriminatory laws did not demand the attention that was required of earlier generations. Viewed in this way, the consciousness raising activities of the 'new' movement represent a form of continuity with the old: rather than being the first women's liberation movement, the movement of the 1960s was an extension of women's activities, able to build on the gains that had already been achieved and able to concentrate on the sexism inherent in daily life, and human relationships.

This new emphasis, however, was not a gradual transition: the women's liberation movement really did 'burst upon the scene'.

The women's liberation movement of the late 1960s came as something of a shock to Constance Rover. 'It was such a radical change,' she said, 'we hadn't known it was coming and it did so much to revitalise the women's movement. Of course,' she added, 'one shouldn't really have been surprised by it. It had happened before in a way. I think some of us who had thought we *were* the women's movement and that the movement was the only form it could have been, must have felt with the new movement a bit the same way as Millicent Garrett Fawcett felt when the Suffragettes were born. After all, she had been working away on women's suffrage for almost forty years and thought that the way she went about it was the only way it could be. And then she woke up one morning to find women's suffrage a major news item, Christabel Pankhurst and Annie Kenney in gaol, and in the headlines, – and a whole new framework and new interest for women's suffrage. It must have been quite a shock for her – she must have had to rethink a bit. But then she came out publicly and said – certainly in the early stages – what a service the women had done for the cause. They had put life back into the suffrage movement. And I feel very much the same about the modern movement. I welcomed it' (1982).

Neither of us could, however, account for the emergence of the women's movement at the time that it appeared. Why then? There was Betty Friedan's book (*The Feminine Mystique*, 1963) – but that only leads to the question of why it was so popular, why it matched so well with women's lives? Simone de Beauvoir's book, *The Second Sex* (1949) was equally if not more radical, but it hadn't led to a feminist renaissance. There was the fact that more married women were in the paid workforce, with more economic freedom, and more conflicts! But again, they had been moving back into the workforce in the fifties and in 1953, Mirra Komarovsky had written about the contradictions for girls, between being educated and not using it after marriage, while in 1956 Alva Myrdal and Viola Klein had written about the contradictions for women between paid work and home (*Women's Two Roles*), and each was probably as significant and perhaps more substantive than *The Feminine Mystique* – but they hadn't caused a revolution either!

Undoubtedly the women's liberation movement in America had strong links with the civil rights movement – in much the same way as it had over a century before when the sisters Sarah and Angelina Grimké had raised their voices to protest about slavery and quickly found they had to use them to defend themselves. The Grimké sisters – and Lucy Stone, to name but a few, – fought for the human rights of slaves and in the process came to recognise they had few of their own.

When women in the civil rights movement, the anti-war movement, and the new left in the United States in the 1960s realised their function was to make tea, not policy, and that their role was to service men ('The only place for women in the movement is prone'), then like their foremothers they began to see that the envisaged *new* social order, contained many features of the *old*, and that the plans for full human rights did not include women! Understandably they objected.

This, however, still doesn't seem to adequately explain the sudden growth of the women's liberation movement – particularly in other Western countries, where there was no equivalent to the civil rights movement – nor does it explain in full the specific form that it took. Although perhaps it is not such a big leap from refusing to service men in the movement to refusing to service men in the home. And domestic labour – and its sexual inequities – was a prime focus of the early stages of the women's liberation movement.

'Men have had a greater range of options open to them,' Constance Rover said, 'particularly when it comes to domestic work. It *has* been possible – and still might be possible – for a man to be considered a *good* husband, even if he made no contribution whatsoever to the housework. But being a *good* wife is very different and a much more restrictive role. The rules are quite clear and quite rigid. Women have never had the same leeway as men and I think the protest about housework was as much a protest about the restrictions it placed on women's behaviour and identity, as it was about women doing more than their fair share of the domestic work' (1982).

When I asked whether she thought there had been any resolution of the battle of the housework, she replied rather humorously that she thought women had probably achieved *conditional* liberation.

'Women have been emancipated on condition that they don't upset men, or interfere too much with men's way of life,' she said and we discussed the number of cases we knew where a man had said 'Of course you can go to work dear – on condition that the children aren't neglected, the meals are still on time, the house is kept in order, and I don't suffer. . . .'

'And that,' said Constance Rover, 'just isn't possible. In fact, it is debatable in many cases whether women have *solved* some of the problems of doing more than their fair share of the work. Perhaps historians will look back on this period and conclude that many women simply took on more new work without shedding much of the old' (1982).

'If it occurs to them to study women,' I replied.

But 'conditional emancipation' is one way of looking at the contradictions of women's supposed gains, and Constance Rover has provided an excellent illustration.

Three Meals a Day

Women's intellect, who wants it?
Not her nearest, not her dearest.
They all want three meals a day.
It's hard to say them nay.

Why not accept the retardation
Of complete domestication –
The gas chamber of the mind
To which women are consigned?

'They also serve who only stand and waite'
But they deserve a better fate

In these days of liberation,
Conditional emancipation,
At least there's toleration
A little learning adds distinction
Gives rise to some congratulation
Always provided (need one say?)
There are still three meals a day

(Constance Rover, *Women Speaking*, April/June, 1981, p.6)

'There was a survey conducted recently in Canada,' I said, 'and they asked men what they were looking for in a woman. All the traditional and expected things came out – "attractive", good wife and mother, intellectual companion – plus the additional feature that they wanted someone who had training and a job – "a little career" some of them said – and who could contribute to the family coffers, without unduly challenging male "sucess" of course.'

'At least in the "old" days,' I added, 'women may have been responsible for the housework but theoretically men were the breadwinners. Working-class women have almost always had two jobs, while men have had only one, and I thought that *liberation* would mean that there would be a more equitable distribution of labour. But now it seems middle-class women also have two jobs while many men still only have one. Women may have moved into accepting financial responsibility for the family – and so many women are solely responsible financially for their families – but again, men haven't moved with the same speed and alacrity into accepting responsibility in the domestic realm. Do you think things could actually be worse, instead of better?' I asked.

The answer was an emphatic NO! 'These things are relative,' Constance Rover reminded me. 'It might seem to you that most men don't do their fair share in the house, but I assure you, in comparison to what they *used* to do, there has been a social revolution. From where I sit, conditional liberation looks a lot better than no liberation at all.'

She talked of the ideology of masculinity, of how short is the distance that men can travel into women's domain without being 'contaminated'. 'It is an ideology which still needs attacking, vigorously,' she said, 'but it is still one which has changed.'

Constance Rover too referred to recent research where some women had indicated that they did not like men 'helping' in the house, that they perceived it as their domain and were threatened when men tried to enter. Given that almost every area women have carved out for themselves and made a power base, men have moved in and taken over – they are disproportionately the *senior* figures in librarianship, nursing, and in the teaching of young children – one could hardly suggest that the women's fears were unfounded. After all, women are only cooks, but when men come into the area, they are chefs! But still we thought it was regrettable that women's space in the world could be so confined that they could become protective about their kitchens. And we also acknowledged that by proving their indispensability many women hope to guarantee their economic survival. If marriage has been made an occupation – and for many women there was the encouragement to see marriage as the *only* occupation available – then it can be threatening to be made redundant, to be shown that *he* can cook and clean – and quite often can accompany it with a rebuff that he can do it more efficiently than she can.

'But these things take time to change,' said Constance Rover, referring to beliefs and attitudes, 'they can only be changed stage by stage.'

'Well,' I said, 'the women's liberation movement has been going on for quite a long time. For centuries. I'm getting impatient. How much longer do you think we will have to wait?'

'It's not all the *one* movement,' she replied; 'You have to make distinctions. There are changes in laws, and changes in attitudes, and they are not always one and the same thing,' and once more she returned to historical examples.

'When it came to the vote, the Suffragettes got impatient. They could see that the struggle had been going on for quite a long time and that they were no closer to getting the vote than when it all started. Some of them even thought they were in a weaker position than when the movement had begun, because during those forty years the anti-feminist forces had the time and opportunity to organise themselves.[1] And Christabel Pankhurst was impatient. She said it was degrading for women to keep asking, and to keep being refused. She wanted action, and a quick resolution to the issue of the vote, that's why she insisted on *Deeds Not Words*.'

I could see what Constance Rover meant about distinguishing between laws and attitudes. The other slogan for which Christabel Pankhurst was famous was *Votes for Women and Chastity for Men*, and obtaining the vote for women was probably a relatively simple matter in comparison to curbing the sexual appetite of men.

And then we were into the issue of women's sexuality and the way it has so often been used against them. 'It doesn't really matter what form women's sexualiy takes,' I said, 'it can be used to discredit them. Mary Wollstonecraft was "too much" – she was called promiscuous, and dismissed: and Christabel Pankhurst was "too little" and she was called a prude, and dismissed. And yet Mary Wollstonecraft was an extremely moral and serious person, and Christabel Pankhurst was making a serious and political point about male sexual demands. But whether you do, or you don't engage in heterosexual activity, either way you are suspect and can be derided in a male dominated world. And the irony is that both Mary Wollstonecraft and Christabel Pankhurst knew that!'

Sexuality is a complex issue – not least because men have defined the terms and appropriated a positive role for themselves, classifying women as objects to meet their needs. One result of this is that there are only two descriptions available for women's sexuality and they are neither enhancing nor helpful: in relation to a man a woman can be too much ('nymphomania') or too little ('frigidity') and both suggest a form of neurosis or aberration. But there is *no* neutral or positive state for women[2] and there *is* a readily available rationale for bringing women into disrepute – no matter what they do! Under the circumstances it is hardly surprising that sexuality should have often proved to be a stumbling block for feminists, and that priority should have frequently been given to developing a meaningful female sexuality *outside* the range of prevailing definitions.

Constance Rover has for many years recognised the central role played by sexuality in the feminist cause – and she has recognised the way sexuality – and 'public morality' – has been used against feminism: it is part of the thesis of her book *Love, Morals and the Feminists*, in which she focuses on sexual morality as an enemy in women's struggle for emancipation.

'So long as women were judged solely on whether they conformed to accepted moral standards,' she had written, 'other qualities of personality or intellect being more or less irrelevant, they had no real hope of emancipation or equality. Men have always accepted the fact that it would be impossible to do business if an inquisition into private morals needed to be held before any negotiation could take place and although, in politics, a surface respectability has usually been required, quite a lot of private irregularity has been overlooked, so long as open scandal could be avoided. This is not to suggest that licentiousness is desirable but that there are many other human qualities, apart from conventional respectability, which are rightly valued amongst men' (1970, p. 4).

For women to be judged according to a double standard of conventional sexual morality is by no means a phenomenon of the past however. The manifestation may have changed but the value system persists. This is why the campaign against sexual harassment has been organised, for women are protesting about being perceived in sexual terms – particularly at the work place – while their work, their personal or intellectual qualities, are treated as irrelevant. Men still define women as sexual objects in relation to themselves, and still exact penalties from women, regardless of the way women behave.

'Women can be damned if they do, and damned if they don't, in the same way as they have been damned historically,' I said. 'The woman who is obliged to grant sexual favours in order to secure or keep her job *is* damned. But so is the woman who refuses. And, of course, as Catherine MacKinnon has pointed out, either way, women's jobs are in jeopardy. She sees sexual harassment as intimidation, as one of the crucial means of undermining women's job security, of putting them in the category of the "reserve" labour force, of keeping women at the bottom rungs of the occupational ladder.'

My analysis of sexual harassment as an extension of rather than a significant change from the harassment endured by women in earlier times, gave Constance Rover little joy. She had thought that 'morality' – as she called it, and 'sexuality' as I called it – was not the weapon that it used to be, and that today women *did* have more opportunities to be valued in terms of their human and creative qualities and not judged in terms of their sex. 'These things are relative, I know,' she said, 'and I can understand that although the *form* may have changed – and it cannot be denied that young women today have considerably more freedom than their Victorian predecessors – although the behaviour might be different, the double standard may be as prevalent and powerful as ever.'

I did not wish to depress Constance Rover, nor to dash her hopes of progress, but I could not refrain from telling her about some of my experiences interviewing sixteen year olds, where it became quite clear that there was one rule for boys and another for girls. 'Most of the boys I talked to genuinely believed that girls existed in relation to their needs and were "available",' I said. 'The boys' role was to play one-up-manship and to be able to boast of their conquests – whether or not they were "successful". Their prowess was a major source of prestige among their peers.

'The double-standard was there for all the world to see – and no less vicious than it was twenty years ago when I was a teenager – despite feminism,' I told her. 'There were two things that just shocked me to the core. One was that girls who were available were called "slags" – evidently because they were seen as "having a reputation", and yet the girls who were *not* "available" were also frequently called "slags" – because of their unco-operative behaviour. The girls were damned if they did, and damned if they didn't, and there was no way out.

'The other thing which shocked me was the overriding contempt that most of the males had for females. I can remember reading *The Female Eunuch* in which Germaine

Greer says that women do not know or will not admit the extent of contempt and hatred that so many men have for women. No woman could have listened to those sixteen year olds and not known. It was frightening. And it's one of the reasons that I cannot accept that there have been fundamental changes, that there is overall progress, and that the future will be better. These boys were the future and all I could see for many women was exploitation, brutality, and oppression.'

Talking about this aspect of male behaviour – and the absolute necessity of feminism as a force of resistance – can quickly lead to feelings of despair, which is probably one of the reasons that it is not often spoken about. There is – and has been – a tendency to gloss over some of the more naked and horrendous features of male power, to ignore the conflict of interest that exists between the sexes, and even to rationalise that things are better now. Constance Rover and I went back to some of the historical examples where women had stated that there would be change – because now there was a new breed of young men raised by feminist mothers. 'Charlotte Perkins Gilman declared at the beginning of the century that the next generation would have all the answers because they had been raised by mothers who valued being female and who insisted on equal human rights,' I said, 'And Betty Friedan is arguing much the same today, that we have a new breed of young men who have put aside their contempt for women and their aggression, and are seeking *partners*. Personally,' I added, 'I don't think Betty Friedan has got any more evidence than Charlotte Perkins Gilman had.'

Apart from sheer survival there is yet another reason that women have often 'chosen' to look on the brighter side of things and to camouflage some of the male contempt towards women. It may have been part of the double-standard for females to have been reared as polite and to have been given the task of being cheerful, of keeping things nice and pleasant when it comes to human relationships, but having been obliged to behave in this way, women have also come to appreciate its value. They have learnt its advantages: it is a more satisfactory way of operating in the world and they are therefore reluctant to abandon it for more confrontational tactics.

And pointing to the harassment, violence and contempt that many men have displayed towards women, *is* to be confrontational. It is not nice, it is not pleasant, it is not cheerful and it doesn't help relationships to run smoothly if women persistently draw attention to the hostile behaviour of men towards women. In fact, there are penalties for women who bring up this topic: now as in the past they will all too frequently find themselves the recipients of *further* harassment, and will probably be called man-haters.

We were both fully aware that there is another double standard, and that the hostile behaviour of men towards women is not called woman-hating. 'There's not even a word for it,' I said with disgust at the blatant hypocrisy. 'I know,' she replied, 'it's grossly unfair. Misogyny is taken for granted, but what would the converse be? Misoandry? Hardly a common and readily understood word' (1982).

In 1970 she had written that the 'anti-man' charge levelled against women is extremely awkward to deal with for 'the difficulty arises that the feminists could hardly challenge male supremacy without attacking men': she then went on to add that 'This raises the question of why it is a heinous offence for a woman to dislike men but . . . has been quite acceptable, even creditable, for a man to say "he has no time for women" ' (p. 146). There is much more anti-women literature than anti-man literature – as feminists have been pointing out over a long period of time – and yet the accusation that feminists are man-haters is still used, and still used as a form of intimidation against women.

'All those anti-women books,' I said to Constance Rover, 'from some of the male pillars of society, and the woman-hating is *never* used to call the worth of *their* work – or of themselves – into question. I haven't noticed any pillars of the establishment saying you can't trust Freud because he's a woman-hater, or that Arnold Bennett was a poor writer because he mixed politics and art when he brought in woman-hating. But that's what was said about Charlotte Perkins Gilman – that her theories were unreliable because they were distorted by man-hating: and that's what they said about Cicely Hamilton, and Elizabeth Robins, and Virginia Woolf – and what is still often said about feminist writers today – that they are "bad" writers, they are propagandists not artists, or polemicists not scholars because they bring in their man-hating.'

We talked about some of the research I was currently doing on the reviews of women's books and I subjected Constance Rover to a detailed account of some of the vicious and sexist practices that often pass for witty and clever reviews: 'I had known that it was unfair,' she commented, 'but I hadn't realised it was as bad as you are portraying it. And I certainly hadn't suspected there were so *few* reviews of women's books' (1982).

'It's like women's talk,' I replied, 'when a woman talks it is so visible – because the "desirable" woman is usually the one who is silent! And a review of a woman's book is so visible when there's an underlying prejudice in society against women being there in the public domain at all!"

We talked about what we might do if we were in charge of reviews of books. Constance Rover was much kinder than I, but nonetheless we agreed that a few of the current male writers in vogue wouldn't get an airing in our pages. And quite a few male reviewers would be out of a job because of their woman-hating bias. 'We tend to forget,' she said, 'just how much control men *do* have over what we know. It really can be quite distressing to think about it.'

That we have so many anti-women books and so few protests from men about them and their distortions, is to Constance Rover nothing other than an illustration that men have been the dominant sex, and in the past have been more literate and have therefore been able to be offensive if they felt like it – without fear of reprisals.

'Often, women-hating can even be seen as a source of humour,' I commented and I was beginning to feel my blood start to boil. 'It's hostility and contempt that is the basis for so many "jokes" about women. And if I don't find them funny, if feminists don't laugh at vicious "jokes" about women, we are condemned again – we are informed that we have no sense of humour! What sort of a society is it,' I asked, 'where men find cruel and dehumanised "jokes" about women funny, but find little about themselves funny? It is a strange and unbalanced society where woman-hating is a high status activity, and where those who do not join in are condemned for their "inadequacies".'

Yet this, we agreed, was characteristic of a patriarchal society; when it came to men's contempt for and mockery of women – well, things haven't changed much since the Middle Ages!

'Men as the dominant sex have always been able to make up the rules,' said Constance Rover, 'and they have usually made them up to their own advantage in relation to women. And feminists, past and present, have had to deal with this. If it wasn't that a feminist was a "man-hater" then it had to be because she "couldn't get a man" that she protested against male power. How else could men explain the behaviour of feminists? The alternative was to admit that women had a genuine grievance against men – and that wouldn't be a very *safe* stand for them to take.'

'Patriarchy,' I replied, 'relies heavily on finding something wrong with the women rather than examining the role of the men. What's *wrong* with women may vary from one generation to the next, but the practice of *blaming* women is as old as patriarchy itself. I am sure Eve would understand,' I said to Constance Rover, trying to find a 'lighter note' for our conversation.

Constance Rover started to talk about some of the women of the past on whom she had done so much research and writing, and as they became 'alive' to me I found it a moving experience. Never before had I sat and listened to tales of my foremothers and it was a delight, and a strength. Sometimes I think we forget what richness men have created for themselves with their myths and legends of positive males from the past: the young boy is initiated into a culture where images of heroes abound, where there are countless examples from the past to offer guidance and esteem. And while boys learn one thing from Moses to King Arthur, from William the Conqueror to Captain Cook, from Aristotle, to Darwin – girls learn quite another! Boys learn that they have an active and visible past in which the male has influenced the environment – girls learn that they have no past, that they are invisible. And yet as so many feminist scholars have shown, from Matilda Joslyn Gage to Margaret Alic, this absence of women is not because women have not made their mark, but because men have rubbed it out!

As Louise Bernikow (1980) has said, imagine what it would be like to grow up as a girl and to be fed myths and legends full of brave, innovative, creative, adventurous and responsible women. What if there was a wealth of tales which began 'Once upon a time there was a woman making an important journey and she came to a crossroad where she met another wise and educated woman who was also making a journey . . .' So simple: so enriching, and yet so rare as to be almost unimaginable. It is men who make the journeys, meet people, have adventures – presumably the women are 'at home' – if they exist at all!

Listening to Constance Rover talk about Mary Wollstonecraft and Josephine Butler, about Anna Wheeler and Annie Besant, about Barbara Bodichon and Frances Power Cobbe was sheer joy – and something that no girl should be denied. Constance Rover knew personal details of these women, was able to relate anecdotes, could talk informatively and entertainingly about their work, their ideas, their visions of the future. All this she had gleaned through her own research – and without the support of the present women's movement – and she had put it to such powerful use by helping to reconstruct women's past, so that other women could share it.

She began where we had left off with the charge levelled at the Suffragettes, that their behaviour was the result of sexual frustration, that they could find no men foolish enough to wed them and so they took to being nuisances out of vexation and with a particular 'sour grapes' philosophy: 'The constant implication that all suffragettes, whether married or single, were in need of a man, must have been a sore trial to them,' Constance Rover had written, and 'even their clashes with authority were said to be for the purpose of embracing a policeman' (1967b, p. 50).

I was outraged, of course, that women's political struggle could be belittled in this way, and I knew that some of the Suffragettes' clashes with the police had been just as brutal –

if not more brutal – than some of the 'incidents' that happen in contemporary times.[3] And I was also angered that it was just so easy for men to cast women into disrepute – it only took a little verbal harassment for men to gain the ascendancy.

'It's another case of no matter what women do, they are damned,' I said, 'If they were single, then they couldn't get a man. But if they were married – particularly to a man who was supportive – then he was likely to be accused of not being a *proper* man, because he failed to comply with the rules of the male supremacist club. It was what happened to Josephine Butler,' I added, 'for her husband *did* support her and that was used against him. It was evidence that he couldn't control his wife and therefore doubts were cast on his ability to do his work and to "control" the boys, his pupils.'

That the pattern of patriarchal ploys has varied little was something we both acknowledged. Today there is still the likelihood that a profeminist male will be considered not a proper male and that he will have to forgo the privileges of male company because of his failure to uphold the rules. Men who do not display contempt for women, who listen to women and accept the legitimacy of women's protest – and there are a rare few – are often perceived as 'henpecked', and isolated from male company. Our ideas about improvement and progress sometimes seem to have little substance.

'There's always the "evidence" that male experts can produce to prove that they are right, and women are wrong,' said Constance Rover, and she quoted some of the same examples that Rebecca West had used. 'There was that Almroth Wright who wrote to *The Times*[4] about the window breaking of the Suffragettes, and called it "Insurgent Hysteria". He implied that the women couldn't be taken seriously because so many of them were in "middle life" and were therefore mentally disturbed. And *his* opinion was "expert medical opinion". And was so hard to refute. The best the women could do at the time was to try and find another "expert" to contradict him. But, of course, by then the damage is done, the link is made, and it's so hard to dislodge the myth' (1982).

'Besides,' I added, 'I bet Almroth Wright got front page

treatment for his derogatory comments about women. If the Suffragettes could have found an expert to contradict him, you can be assured it would have been carried in small print in one paragraph in an obscure place in the newspaper.'

Experts on women – who are not women – have been more than plentiful as Virginia Woolf and Barbara Ehrenreich and Deirdre English (1978) have observed, and it is interesting to note how many of their scientific pronouncements have been refuted by later generations – for few of us today for example subscribe to the belief that the education of girls leads to atrophy of the uterus and the likelihood that their brains will burst, and yet as Carol Dyhouse (1981) has pointed out this *was* a widely held scientific precept a century ago. That there has been so much science that has later been exposed as nothing other than male prejudice has led at times to questions being raised: is there something wrong with the men who practise it or something fundamentally wrong with our belief about science as an objective body of knowledge which is free from prejudice?

There is one school of thought which settles for the former and declares that the men who put forward their prejudices as scientific fact, were not proper scientists. But there is another school of thought – and the feminist scientist Ruth Hubbard (among others) is prominent within it – which is inclined to the belief that it *was* science that these misogynistic males were practising, not pseudo-science. Ruth Hubbard argues that there is no value-free and objective science and that all science is built upon the assumptions of the people who engage in it – and in a patriarchal society that means that science is built upon the devaluation of women – and it did, and still does frequently show.

'Do you think this is one area where contemporary feminists have made gains?' I asked Constance Rover, recalling how women like Matilda Joslyn Gage and Charlotte Perkins Gilman had put so much faith in science as an objective and value-free body of knowledge, and how women like Rita Arditti and Ruth Hubbard were now arguing that science – like all other institutions in our society – is the product of patriarchal values and can therefore be used against women. 'Do you think we are beginning to assert our own authority and to reject the idea that men are the experts? It was a real joy to me,' I added 'when I discovered Adrienne Rich's words that men are not the authoritative sex, and that objectivity is simply the name that men have given their own subjectivity. And I loved reading Matilda Joslyn Gage's words that far from being the rational sex men showed a distinct propensity for "ungovernable frenzy".'

'By the way,' I continued, 'I've always found that the best evidence of male irrationality and frenzy can be produced if you suggest to some males that *reason* is simply the name they use for their own *emotions*.'

While I was prepared to believe that women had made some gains in the intellectual realm and were today more likely to insist on the validity of their own experience and the legitimacy of their own reason – even if they were not treated seriously by men – Constance Rover was not quite so ready to believe that great strides had been made. Consciousness raising groups, women's studies courses and feminist books and programmes had all helped, of course, to substantiate women's view of the world and to give women confidence to assert it. But there was still an intellectual double standard operating which permitted men to be the owners of ideas and theories, which allowed men to be the genuine thinkers. Women were still frequently seen to be governed by intuition and not to have the same capacity for logic as men.

'There have been many women who have disputed the evidence and theories of the male experts,' said Constance Rover, 'there have been so many women who have challenged men's right to make pronouncements on women, as well as challenging the pronouncements themselves. Think of Mary Wollstonecraft,' she reminded me, 'a woman could not have been intellectually more audacious and challenging than she was. She held up some of the intellectual giants of the time – like Rousseau for example – and completely repudiated their arguments. She showed that their theories were just male prejudice and had nothing to do with so called logic. She did almost two hundred years ago what so many women are doing today.'

And I remembered Mary Wollstonecraft's resounding

words: *'Who made man the exclusive judge?'* I remembered that women's protest against male power and authority had been going on for a very long time.

Constance Rover's familiarity with and understanding of women of the past created for me an almost magic atmosphere: it was as if these women had lived yesterday – or as if they might suddenly just walk through the door. We talked about them as though they were personal acquaintances and friends, and I realised that never before had I had such a discussion where the conversation went back and forth about Mary and Millicent, Josephine and Christabel. Never before had I felt myself so much part of a tradition.

'It was fundamental to Mary Wollstonecraft that women be taken seriously as intellectual beings,' said Constance Rover; 'she wanted them to be the intellectual equals of men which is why she placed so much faith in education. When men were educated and women were not, you couldn't *expect* women to be treated seriously. But when both sexes were educated, it would be a different matter: at least that's what she believed as did so many women who came after her.

'But,' added Constance Rover, 'Mary Wollstonecraft is a classic example of the way sexual morality has been used against women. It's not surprising that people may not know of her explanations and her theories, because it is her sexuality, her promiscuity and "irregularities" which have received all the attention and for which she is primarily known. Her feminist arguments and her theories on education have often gone unnoticed, and yet she was one of the most prominent and influential intellectuals of her time' (1982).

And it wasn't just against herself that Mary Wollstonecraft's sexuality was used: she was held up as an undesirable and unfortunate example, and after her, generations of feminists confronted the daunting task of trying to 'put right' what a male dominated society decreed Mary Wollstonecraft had 'put wrong'!

'Mary Wollstonecraft,' continued Constance Rover, 'was used to make a connection between feminism and immorality. There was the suggestion that only immoral women would make the sort of protest that she did and so many women were dissuaded from identifying with feminism. It was very important for women to appear "moral" in those times – after all, their reputations were really all they had for not many of them would have had the courage to pursue the independent life that Wollstonecraft did – and so they couldn't afford to be associated with the feminist cause, because the price of appearing immoral was too high. If a woman lost her reputation, she lost everything because that was the main yardstick for her value in society. Of course Wollstonecraft understood that – it was one of the main things she objected to, but that didn't prevent women from being discouraged from joining the feminist ranks. And it didn't protect other women either because for years after-wards – even a century afterwards – feminists were still trying to live down the reputation that had been created for Wollstonecraft.'

'I'd call it plain intimidation,' I said, 'another example of sexual harassment. It's part of women's history and we should be studying it more closely.'

'I agree,' said Constance Rover, 'that's partly why I did the research that I did. It doesn't matter what you call it, there's no denying that it was decidedly effective and that it is one of the powerful enemies that feminists have had to deal with. The generations of women who came after Mary Wollstonecraft had to spend a lot of time and energy refuting the allegations of immorality and convincing society that they were decent, respectable and highly moral women.'

And this is one of the reasons that when referred to, they can today be represented as dull and even reactionary.

'Having to put so much time into defending themselves against charges of immorality would have drained them of the energy which could otherwise have been directed towards resistance,' I said, 'and it also had its own penalties because they were so intent to prove how pure and respectable they were, that some of them backed themselves into the corner of suggesting that they had no sexuality at all. That was the position Dora Russell was so critical of,' I added.

But their caution is understandable. In their terms there were virtually no alternatives. 'One may not like it but one can appreciate why Millicent Garrett Fawcett thought it necessary to dissociate herself from Mary Wollstonecraft's "morals" when she wrote the Introduction to the 1891 edition of *A Vindication of the Rights of Women*' said Constance Rover (1982): 'In unravelling the curious tangle of relationships, intrigues, suicides and attempted suicides of the remarkable group of personalities to whom Mary Wollstonecraft belonged,' Millicent Garrett Fawcett had written, 'one is sickened for ever . . . of the subject of irregular relations' (quoted in Rover, 1970, p. 53).

'Not only did she think it necessary to dissociate herself from Wollstonecraft,' Constance Rover added, 'she thought it necessary to demonstrate disapproval. She joined in the conventional condemnation of Mary's relationship with Gilbert Imlay, she showed a distinct absence of sympathy for the desperate straits in which Mary found herself and which led her to attempt suicide, and Mrs Fawcett helped to imply that Mary was somehow responsible for the tragedies which occurred after her death – particularly in relation to her daughters' (1982).

Hardly sisterly I had to agree, but then Millicent Garrett Fawcett was doing what she thought was best: she was trying to present the case for women in the best possible – and most convincing – light!

'She might have dissociated herself from Mary Wollstonecraft,' Constance Rover reminded me, 'but at the same time you have to remember that she was responsible for putting Wollstonecraft's ideas before the public once more – after almost a century of neglect. She *did* want feminists to know what Wollstonecraft had to say and because she wrote the Introduction, Millicent Garrett Fawcett gave those ideas validity and endorsement. Some of Mrs Fawcett's ideas wouldn't go down too well today though,' Constance Rover added. 'One of the reasons she gives for wanting to reclaim Wollstonecraft was that part of her virtue lay in her insistence on women's domestic labour as a duty' (1982).

As far as many of the nineteenth-century British feminists could see Mary Wollstonecraft was not in the public eye and was not taken seriously because she could be discredited sexually, and it did seem as though she had frightened women away from the feminist cause. One thing Millicent

Garrett Fawcett – and Lydia Becker and Emily Davies among others – wanted, was to be taken seriously: they wanted public attention for their campaign and they wanted to win more women to their ranks. So it seemed that if they were to learn the lesson provided by Mary Wollstonecraft, they would have to avoid even the faintest breath of scandal: their behaviour would have to be above reproach and demonstrably of the most decent and virtuous kind.

'There were so many women in the women's movement that it really is surprising that they did stay so free of scandal,' said Constance Rover. 'There was no British equivalent to Victoria Woodhull, the American feminist, who was associated with free love and who was involved in exposing the scandalous behaviour of Henry Ward Beecher, one of the most reputable men of society' (1982).

'I think there was quite a lot of pressure exerted at times,' I replied; 'when Elizabeth Wolstenholme, a fairly prominent feminist, decided to live with Mr Elmy without "benefit of clergy" on the grounds that no decent feminist would get married and become her husband's property, some of her friends were on the doorstep pretty quickly. They told her that she had to get married – on feminist grounds – because the movement couldn't afford any scandals or any association with "free love". What was good for the women's movement was thought to be good for the individuals within it.'

'The feminists were all terribly concerned about not frightening people away,' said Constance Rover, 'they didn't want to frighten women – but they didn't want to frighten men either. They thought they had to win men over to their cause if women were to get the vote and so naturally they tried to establish good relationships with men' (1982).

'Both Christabel and Millicent used to complain that if women had votes it would be easy enough to get votes,' I added, 'but when women did *not* have votes and the only way for them to get votes was for men to agree that it was a good idea, the task looked to be a pretty difficult one. No wonder Millicent went to such great lengths to reassure men that nothing would change *after* women got the vote, that they would still be womanly and do the housework. I don't think she would have had a very receptive male audience if she had informed men that there would be a social revolution, after women got the vote, and that it would be the beginning of women competing for men's jobs, and the end of women doing the housework.'

There is no puzzle about why women adopted the position that they did: to them the only plausible strategy seemed to be to act in a reassuring way and to display their impeccable moral standards for all the world to see. They didn't understand that in the long term it really didn't matter how they conducted themselves, for in the words of Elizabeth Cady Stanton, the worth of women's actions resided in the women and not the actions, in a patriarchal world.

The very respectability of these feminists has been repeatedly used against them. Teresa Billington Greig – one of the Suffragettes and a founder of the Women's Freedom League – maintained that the respectable feminists were behaving in precisely the way that men wished them to, and that as the women in the suffrage movement caused no trouble at all, men could go on accommodating their polite requests – for centuries if need be! And of course today there are few flattering profiles of some of those respectable feminists: with the portraits that we have received of them we too tend to be harsh in our judgments.

But the nineteenth-century feminists were acting in a way that they thought would produce the greatest gains for women. They really did believe that if men had nothing to be frightened of, women would be able to steer a safe path through the patriarchal minefield. They really did take men at their word, that they were *just* creatures, interested in fair play and would therefore soon see the error of unequal ways and would be only too pleased and willing to make changes. It was the women who came afterwards who identified the conflict of interest, who insisted that no one ever gave up power because they were asked nicely, who called men the enemy and declared the sex-war. To the nineteenth-century feminists such strategies were unthinkable – and perhaps they were right in their time. The success of the Suffragettes was based on the fact that there were just so many of them, it was a mass movement, a popular cause. Even if one could imagine Millicent Garrett Fawcett and Lydia Beeker 'calling the troops to battle stations', there is every chance that no one would have come.

For the nineteenth-century feminists it seemed as though there was no other way but to play within the rules.

'Take Emily Davies, for example,' I said – who along with Barbara Bodichon[5] was one of the founders of Girton, 'she has been portrayed as positively fanatical in her requirements of her women students. But she recognised that they *were* behaving in a radical fashion simply by challenging the fundamental prejudice that women were intellectually inferior and therefore did not warrant an education. She knew that the students were being watched like hawks for any lapses that could be cited as evidence that education was damaging for women, and she wasn't going to risk that. She wasn't going to have the entire enterprise collapse because of the irresponsible or unthinking behaviour of one of the students – so she insisted on the strictest rules.'

'She thought those rules and regulations were absolutely necessary,' said Constance Rover, 'and indeed, they probably were. They certainly helped open up higher education to women. Emily Davies spent virtually her entire adult life in the campaign and she did achieve success.'

And there were numerous obstacles placed in her path, and at least one dozen good reasons that she should be unsuccessful! Many Cambridge dons were determined that women would never enter their sanctuary and they did not defend their territory by mere polite debate. There were real battles at Cambridge – despite the fact that male historians have not chosen to enter them in the records.[6]

Emily Davies's campaign wasn't helped by the fact that she was dealing with an irrational and emotional foe, either: 'Some of the great dons argued at one and the same time that women's presence in the halls of learning would be the cause of *unsexing* women and the cause of *distracting* men,' I said exasperatedly 'and it was just another case of women being damned if they were "feminine", and damned if they were not. And Emily Davies just kept on and on until they opened the door a fraction. It's a shame that she is not seen as a more positive figure today because we really do owe her a lot. Still,'

I added, 'she probably wouldn't care twopence for *how* she was portrayed today. What was important for her was that women should get in . . . and they did.'

What is important to us though is that we are without a history of positive women, if she is portrayed as sufficiently insignificant and unattractive to be worthy of notice.

Because she was so concerned with keeping even the slightest breath of scandal from the campaign for higher education of women, Emily Davies insisted that there should be no links with Josephine Butler's campaigns against the Contagious Diseases Acts – which did invite scandal and notoriety. This doesn't for a minute mean that Emily Davies disapproved of Josephine Butler – or her campaign – for on the contrary there is evidence that many of the highly moral and respectable nineteenth-century feminists were in favour of the repeal of the acts, even if they didn't come out and say so in public. But they thought that support for Josephine Butler might jeopardise the campaigns for suffrage and higher education.[7]

What it does mean is that Emily Davies – and Millicent Garrett Fawcett and many more – had to respond to the circumstances in which they found themselves. They were circumstances which were controlled by men and over which women had little or no influence: they were circumstances for which women cannot be blamed.

'If there's any fault to be found it's on our side,' I said to Constance Rover, 'for not appreciating the limited range of options that were available to women. You have shown just how thoroughly and systematically the prevailing moral code was used against women, and how readily they could be discredited, but how many women of today understand just what our foremothers were up against?' I asked.

'It was a major and continual problem,' she replied, 'and one they were all aware of. They did want changes for women, they wanted education, employment, the vote, and a much wider sphere for women for growth and development. But every time they brought up the issue they could be condemned. As soon as they suggested that there should be more in life for women than being wives and mothers, they were accused of being anti-family. And that,' she added grimly, 'can still happen today. Women have been bedevilled by the definitions of a "proper" and "moral" woman. If they don't challenge these ideas then they are allowing them to continue. But if they do challenge them they invite condemnation' (1982).

'So the only *good* woman,' I said, 'really is the one who conforms to male ideas of what she should be?' 'Unfortunately,' Constance Rover replied, 'that's probably the case.'

By definition then, women who protest or resist, are *bad*.

We turned our attention to some of the bad women of the past, and to the bad press that they have received. I told Constance Rover of Alison Ravetz's research on Mary Wollstonecraft and how she had patiently reconstructed the pieces to show how Wollstonecraft had been completely misrepresented – with her husband playing no small part in the process. 'Alison Ravetz says there is still no serious feminist treatment of Wollstonecraft and her philosophy, and so we are still deprived of her ideas. But there is just so much work to do to reclaim some of these marvellous women. All women should be able to sit and talk like we are doing about our past, we should all be able to discuss the dilemmas of the nineteenth-century feminists, the achievements of the Suffragettes, the ideas of women philosophers and historians, but it's so new, and so strange,' I added, 'that often when I start talking about Josephine's husband, or Frances Power Cobbe's relationships, women just look at me with incredulity. The idea that there hasn't been a past for women is so deeply engrained that some just can't believe that we really have had all these superb women doing so many daring deeds. Besides,' I added, 'it's the same old problem, because women then have to face the fact that it was men who wiped the slate clean – and they didn't do it by accident!'

Constance Rover recognised that many women – even of our relatively recent past – have been very effectively buried. One 'disappearance' which interests her is that of Annie Besant. 'She was the first woman to advocate birth control from a public platform,' Constance Rover informed me, 'and really, it is quite obvious that much of women's emancipation does depend on the ability to prevent pregnancy. Yet she doesn't have a place in feminist history.'

'Richard Carlile plays a role in the story,' she began, 'because of his championship of the free press. He published Tom Paine's *Rights of Man* and *Age of Reason* but his real sin was that he published them *cheaply* and so they were available to the "masses" which was thought to be very dangerous. He was repeatedly fined and imprisoned but he kept on publishing. Did you know,' she asked as a matter of interest, 'that at one stage there were so many publishers and booksellers in Newgate Prison that in 1824 they began to edit the *Newgate Monthly Magazine*? It was published from Carlile's shop' (1982).

And Carlile, apart from advocating the abolition of the monarchy and secular education, also advocated women's liberation and birth control.

'He had a "moral wife", Eliza Sharples,' Constance Rover continued, 'and when he was in gaol, she used to give the lectures on free thought, and women's emancipation under the name of *Isis*: she even produced a journal, the *Isis* in the 1830s. But after *Isis* the next person to advocate birth control in public was Annie Besant. She was a strange woman in many ways – she certainly packed a great deal into her life and her biographer called his first volume on her *The First Five Lives of Annie Besant* and the following volume *The Last Four Lives of Annie Besant*. But even if she did adopt some unusual religious ideas later in her life, her contribution was considerable' (1982).

Of Annie Besant (1847–1933), Constance Rover has written that she has not been given a place as one of the heroines of the women's movement because 'many of the causes she espoused were anathema to the leaders,' and it was particularly the issue of birth control that they found unacceptable. But her 'first formal speech was deliberately made in support of women's enfranchisement. It was good, stirring stuff, demolishing the conventional anti-suffragist arguments.' If the vote was to be withheld from women on the grounds that it would take them from their work, why didn't the same rule apply to men, Annie Besant had asked? The logic of this argument was that it was only safe for idle people to be allowed to vote (Rover, 1970, p. 102).

Annie Besant was a successful and popular speaker: she

was also 'a wife separated from her husband, following a marriage which she felt to be an imprisonment,' and she 'was naturally conscious of the unsatisfactory position of married women both legally and socially. She came to realize this even more acutely when her atheism was used as a reason for depriving her of custody of her daughter' (ibid., p. 103).

With Charles Bradlaugh – who was also a champion of the freedom of the press, an atheist, a republican, and an advocate of birth control, – Annie Besant formed a publishing company which republished the 'Fruits of Philosophy' (a simple pamphlet containing contraceptive advice) and so both were brought to trial in June 1877 on the charge of issuing an obscene publication.

'Both conducted their own defence,' Constance Rover has written, and 'Mrs Besant eloquently pleaded the case for family limitation as a means of relief to the working class woman. . . . The verdict went against them . . . but was reversed on appeal, on technical grounds.' However as neither 'Bradlaugh nor Annie Besant thought highly of . . . *The Fruits of Philosophy* . . . following the trial, Mrs Besant produced a fresh work, *The Law of Population* (1877) which was sold for 6d in pamphlet form. She took the neo-Malthusian view that the relief of poverty necessitated the limitation of working-class families, described the contraceptive methods then available and refuted opponents objections. Like Marie Stopes after her, she wished to help working-class women living in poverty, and felt it unjust that such women should be deprived of knowledge which could contribute to their happiness' (ibid., p. 104).

'Fifty years later Dora Russell was involved in the very same arguments – again,' I said. 'But by then I think there were many women who had managed to resist the idea that birth control was horrendous, part of "prostitute's" law and something no self-respecting woman would have any part of. It makes me furious to think of all that time women were *denied* the necessary knowledge about contraception – and according to Dora Russell it made the women pretty furious in the 1920s. They weren't going to abide by the rules of morality and sexuality any more, they weren't prepared to accept that convenient myth that "nice" girls didn't know about contraception.'

'Well, things changed fairly drastically with the Suffragettes,' stated Constance Rover who sees many parallels between them and the women of the contemporary women's movement. 'The case for respectability and morality was never the same again after the Pankhursts – with all those women breaking windows, heckling members of parliament, going to gaol – and behaving in the most unrespectable and immoral manner. And the issue of morality wasn't the same again after Christabel declared that there was nothing wrong with the morality of women – but a great deal wrong with the morality of men! It was really quite politically astute of Christabel to focus on male behaviour as the problem, even if it did ignore some of the questions that faced women' (1982).

'Rebecca West has said that Christabel's outburst against *male* venereal disease, which was in "the worst possible taste" was "the best possible strategy" for throwing over numerous restrictions placed on women's proper behaviour,' I said. 'The very idea that an "attractive" young woman could bring herself to *mention* such a topic, and insist that men must change if they wanted women – was sufficient to promote apoplexy among many. And when the world didn't end, when Christabel lived to fight another round, it's not surprising that women were prepared to follow her example.'

'It did take both *branches* of the movement to achieve success, you know,' Constance Rover cautioned, and we discussed the deficiencies of the 'one correct strategy' approach and agreed that the more fronts feminism worked on, the stronger it would be. 'It isn't a case of whether the Constitutionalists or the Suffragettes were right or wrong, but that they were both necessary. Mrs Fawcett didn't depart from her position that the vote could be won by "persuasion" and "education" and as the co-operation of an all-male parliament was essential to her plan she was always anxious to provide "face-saving" options for the men. But she was helped immeasurably by Christabel's tactics of applying pressure and making the politicians uncomfortable. The WSPU pressured and the Constitutionalists made the face-saving suggestions and together they were more effective than either could have been singly' (1982).

That's certainly not how they are portrayed however. We are led to believe that the 'division' between the two was an obstacle and not the strength of diversity.

'Mrs Fawcett was of course embarrassed at times and Christabel's outspoken criticism of men did not make her job any easier. I suspect that at times she was mortified by militant actions. There she was trying to win men to the cause and while Christabel has been accused of many things, trying to gain the favour of men wasn't one of them. Christabel didn't tell men that they had nothing to fear. On the contrary part of her strategy was directed towards frightening men, frightening them into granting women the vote She was prepared to demonstrate that their lives would be easier and more comfortable *only* when they had voted for women to vote!'

The different approaches of the Constitutionalists as represented by Millicent Garrett Fawcett, and the Militants as represented by Christabel Pankhurst have their contemporary parallels. There is conciliation or confrontation: should feminists adopt a policy of either/either, neither/neither, or both? It is understandable that women should prefer negotiation to confrontation, co-operation to conflict – but what is the outcome of negotiation between a dominant and oppressed group? 'If we had votes we could get votes,' said our foremothers: and if we had power, we could get power, if we had equality we could get equality. . . . But if a 'combination' of Constitutionalists and Militants worked so well in the past then perhaps it can work again.

That we may not have noticed the 'tandem' nature of the Militants and the Constitutionalists may be due to our own myopia, but it is also partly because they have not been presented to us in this light. Today, both have been 'discredited'. There is no great rush on the libraries for example with eager students desperately wanting to find out more about the fantastic Mrs Fawcett; and in the minds of many, the less said about Christabel Pankhurst, the better. In the long run, the fact that one was respectable and polite and a conciliator, and the other was not, doesn't really count when women have little or no control over their own knowledge. Both women end up in much the same negative place under patriarchy.

Yet in their own time it seems that the penalties for being 'immoral' and 'impolite' were greater than for those who abided by the rules. Mrs Fawcett did not experience the intense harassment that Christabel Pankhurst did when she came out in opposition to men. Christabel was subjected to various forms of harassment as every attempt was made to intimidate and discredit her: one of the most frequent forms (and one still used today) was to accuse her of lesbianism.

'The only thing that might have changed,' I said to Constance Rover, 'is that among women today "lesbianism" doesn't carry the fear that it might have earlier this century. It can still be a difficult issue, of course, but lots of women have come to appreciate its positive connotations. In the last resort it really means that there are women who have arranged their lives so that they are man-free when it comes to personal relations. When there's so much evidence that relationships between the dominant and the oppressed aren't very satisfactory – to say the least – then the decision to dispense with the dominant must be seen as reasonable on purely logical grounds.'

'It also has a political dimension,' stated Constance Rover. 'Obviously there have always been lesbians in the women's movement – as there have always been lesbians in the female population in general – but so far as I know the present is the first time that women have insisted on the *politics* of female independence. If some of the Suffragettes were lesbian, they didn't advertise it. They didn't come out and claim it as part of their politics' (1982).

'But it was patriarchal politics to declare that there was "an outbreak of lesbianism" among the Suffragettes,' was my response. 'It was done to discredit the women, and to undermine their cause. It was another part of the process of labelling them as man-haters in a male controlled society which doesn't understand or doesn't want to accept that it's quite in order to be against men when they behave in an abominable fashion. It's the old story of not being allowed to criticise the rulers although they are allowed to criticise – ad nauseum – those whom they rule.'

In the case of lesbianism, we decided, it was possible that women today had seized the initiative, and claimed lesbianism as a positive, before it could be used against them.

We accepted that it wasn't difficult to see why so many women would perceive it as advantageous to *not* to live with men. 'It usually halves the domestic work load,' I said, 'and it drastically reduces the amount of emotional work demanded of women in conventional heterosexual relationships. If there are *two* adults who are both concerned to keep things running smoothly, who are prepared to do the emotional mending and patching – and listening – then it's not such an enormous job. But when only one does the work, when only one gives, and the other takes, it can be exhausting.'

There was no need to cover the topic of 'the trials of men' with Constance Rover: she had covered it all before – again, in her own novel fashion:

Male Companionship

For the company of men
There is a heavy price to pay,
Boring hours in clubs or pubs
Listening to what they say:

Talk of war or talk of sport,
How the last campaign was fought,
How a ball was kicked or caught.

At last amid smoke and din
With the help of beer or gin
A mild euphoria sets in.

Although the propping up of bars
Is a life-style to deplore
The *Kinder, Küche, Kirche*, role
Is an even greater bore.

'Oh dear,' I said, 'we will probably have the wrath of the male establishment descend upon us, yet we are only doing what so many other women have done – for such a long time.

And we are not only criticising the male life-style, but the confined and restrictive female one as well.'

'There's no safe path through the minefield, even today,' acknowledged Constance Rover.

And so our conversation continued, for many hours as we 'gossipped' about the women of the past who were so real to us. She talked of Anna Wheeler, the illuminating feminist socialist, who had inspired William Thompson's feminist treatise of 1825 – an enlightening book which has been all but overlooked. 'It's because of its title,' I said. 'It must be one of the longest in the English language – *Appeal of One Half of the Human Race, Women, against the Pretensions of the Other Half, Men, to Restrain them in Political and thence in Civil and Domestic Slavery.*'

I talked of Matilda Joslyn Gage, and Mary Beard, of Frances Wright and Ruth Herschberger, and together we wove stories about women's past and made them part of women's present. We were free from the interference of men, outside the range of harassment, and we were not frightened to compare notes, to discuss different interpretations, even to disagree. It is a privilege which men take for granted for themselves but one which is rarely permitted to women.

In that warm room there was enormous security as the parade of positive women went on and on. All women should have such space, such access to this knowledge, such strength that it brings. Through her work Constance Rover has tried to provide that space, that knowledge, that strength. She understands that she is just one of the many women who form that long tradition: she is proud of the part that she has played for unless her words are erased she has helped to provide the evidence that for as long as men have been the dominant sex, there has always been a 'women's movement', even if it has not taken the contemporary form.

'I wonder whether my crime will have been that I was too respectable or too radical?' she asked, 'With "morality" these days, it is rather difficult to tell.'

'While men are the gatekeepers, it doesn't really matter,' I replied. 'The very fact that we are protesting means that either way we are damned.'

'It would be interesting to know what was said about

today's women's movement in fifty years time though,' she said thoughtfully. 'Do you think it will need yet another feminist renaissance to burst upon the scene to revitalise today's feminists?'

If the society that we know is not destroyed by nuclear war, or unemployment, or civil war ... then the question really is whether the younger feminists of today will, in fifty years time, be astonished by the claims of a new generation – that they have *invented* a women's movement. Will we be obliged to remind them that there's always been a women's movement this century?

A note from Constance Rover

I am both flattered and slightly dismayed at Dale's account of me and my work; flattered to have been written about at all (and in such a warm way), also because I can think of many women more worthy than myself to be included; slightly dismayed, because it is almost impossible for another to express one's ideas with exactitude. Although Dale has kindly shown me her text, to go through it and alter it so that it expressed my precise thought would (as we used to say in our Euclid) be absurd. It is her book and what comes through very strongly is her deep commitment to the women's cause, a commitment which I share.

NOTES

Introduction
1 See Sally Roesch Wagner's 1980 'Introduction' to Matilda Joslyn Gage's *Women, Church and State: The Original Exposé of Male Collaboration Against the Female Sex* (1893).
2 For further discussion see Dale Spender (1982b), *Women of Ideas and What Men Have Done to Them: From Aphra Behn to Adrienne Rich*.

1   Hazel Hunkins Hallinan
1 I have used a combination of Hazel Hunkins Hallinan's 1977 address and her more recent comments on it.
2 She frequently used a pseudonym which makes it difficult to locate some of her early writing.
3 Jack Reed, author of *Ten Days that Shook the World* on which the film *Reds* is based.
4 A selection of articles from *Time and Tide* is to be published soon by Pandora Press.
5 The 300 Club aims at getting 300 women into parliament, 'half' the parliamentary population.
6 For further discussion, see Cathy Porter, 1980.
7 For further discussion see Robyn Rowland, 1983, *Women Who Do and Women Who Don't – Join the Women's Movement*.
8 It is questionable whether Mary Wollstonecraft was indeed the first: see Dale Spender, 1982b.

2   Rebecca West
1 Rebecca West discusses male promiscuity in her recent book *1900*, see West, 1982c.
2 See Cheri Davis Langdell, 1983, and Lynne Spender, 1983, for further discussion.
3 The Fawcett Society is currently carrying out a survey to determine how many women writers are presently being studied in literature courses in higher education and preliminary findings are astonishing – there are so few!
4 My own preliminary research on the review sections of *The Observer*, *The Sunday Telegraph* and *The Sunday Times* over the last three years suggests that about 6% of the space is allocated to women's books. If and when women writers are reviewed, they are frequently treated 'en masse'.
5 The 1977 collection of Rebecca West's work contains a bibliography of articles and reviews on West. First of all it is astonishing that so little has been written – fourteen articles since

1923 and this includes reviews and interviews with newspapers – and secondly, apart from a 1966 article by Mary Ellmann, there is no article on West by a feminist entered in this bibliography.

3   Dora Russell

1 Women were not permitted to be full members of Cambridge University until 1948, see Rita McWilliams-Tullberg, 1975.
2 For further discussion see Barbara Strachey, 1980, the daughter of Ray Strachey and the great-niece of Alys Pearsall-Smith Russell.
3 See Amanda Spry, forthcoming, *Who's the Proper Feminist?*
4 See also Hazel Hunkins Hallinan, p. 27–9.
5 This, and other publications of Dora Russell's will be reprinted in the forthcoming *Dora Russell Reader* from Pandora Press.

4   Mary Stott

1 See Phillip Goldberg 1974, and Dale Spender 1982a for further discussion of work signed by men being rated as impressive while the same work signed by women is rated as mediocre.
2 See Davies, 1915, *Maternity: Letters from Working Women*, and 1931, *Life As We Have Known It: By Co-operative Working Women*.

5   Constance Rover

1 This was the view of Teresa Billington-Greig.
2 For further discussion see Dale Spender, 1980, *Man Made Language*.
3 See Caroline Morrell, 1981, *'Black Friday' and Violence against Women in the Suffragette Movement*.
4 *The Times*, 27 March 1912.
5 For further discussion of Barbara Bodichon, see Jacquie Matthews, 1983, and forthcoming.
6 This aspect of women's history which is both exciting and illuminating is covered by some women historians, however; see for example Margaret Bryant 1979, *The Unexpected Revolution* and Rita McWilliams-Tullberg 1975, *Women at Cambridge: A Men's University – Though of a Mixed Type*
7 See Eleanor Reimer, forthcoming.

Fairfield, Letitia, 1928, 'The Need for Birth-Controller Control' *Time and Tide,* vol. 9, no. 23, 8 June, pp. 554–5.

Finch, Anne, 1973, 'Introduction' in Joan Goulianous (ed.), *By a Woman Writ,* New English Library, pp. 71–3.

Flexner, Eleanor, 1979, *Century of Struggle: The Woman's Rights Movement in the United States* (revised edition, first published 1959), Belknap Press and Harvard University Press, Cambridge, Mass.

Friedan, Betty, 1963, *The Feminine Mystique,* W. W. Norton; 1965, Penguin, Harmondsworth, Middlesex.

Gage, Matilda Joslyn, 1893, *Woman, Church and State: The Original Exposé of Male Collaboration Against the Female Sex,* Charles Kerr, Chicago; reprinted 1980, Persephone Press, Watertown, Mass.

Garis, Leslie, 1982, 'Rebecca West and H. G. Wells', *Sydney Morning Herald,* 10 April, pp. 21–2.

Gilman, Charlotte Perkins, 1898, 'The Yellow Wallpaper,' *New England Magazine,* vol. V, January, pp. 647–59: (as Charlotte Perkins Stetson) reprinted Ann J. Lane (ed.), 1981.

The Charlotte Perkins Gilman Reader, The Women's Press, London.

Goldberg, Philip, 1974, 'Are Women Prejudiced Against Women', in Judith Stacey et al. (eds), *And Jill Came Tumbling After: Sexism in American Education,* Dell Publishing, New York, pp. 37–42.

Greer, Germaine, 1970, *The Female Eunuch,* MacGibbon & Kee, London.

Horner, Matina, S., 1974, 'Toward an Understanding of Achievement – related Conflicts in Women', in Judith Stacey et al. (eds) *And Jill Came Tumbling After: Sexism in American Education,* Dell Publishing, New York, pp. 43–62.

Hubbard, Ruth, 1981, 'The Emperor Doesn't Wear Any Clothes: the Impact of Feminism on Biology', in Dale Spender (ed.), *Men's Studies Modified,* Pergamon Press, Oxford, pp. 213–236.

Hunkins Hallinan, Hazel (ed.) 1968, *In Her Own Right: A Discussion Conducted by the Six Point Group* Harrap, London.

Hunkins Hallinan, Hazel, 1977a, Talk to Women's Press Club Washington, D C, 23 August.

Hunkins Hallinan, Hazel, 1977b, Speech delivered at the Memorial Service for Alice Paul, National Cathedral, Washington, D C, 20 July.

Hunkins Hallinan, Hazel, 1982, Interviews with Dale Spender, London, January/February.

Hynes, Samuel, 1977, 'Introduction: In Communion with Reality', in Rebecca West, *A Celebration,* Penguin, Harmondsworth, Middlesex, pp. ix–xviii.

King, Josephine and Mary Stott (eds) 1977, *Is This Your Life? Images of Women in the Media,* Virago, London.

BIBLIOGRAPHY

Alic, Margaret, (forthcoming) *Hypatia's Heritage: History of Women's Science* Pandora Press, London.

Arditti, Rita, et al., (eds), 1980, *Science and Liberation*, Black [Montreal.

Aries, Elizabeth, 1976, 'Interaction patterns and themes of m female, and mixed groups', *Small Group Behaviour*, 7, pp. 17–1

Barrett, Marjorie, 1969, 'One Woman's War', *She*.

Bart Pauline, 1981, 'Seizing the Means of Reproduction: An Ill Feminist Abortion Clinic – How and Why it Worked', in Helen Roberts (ed) *Women, Health and Reproduction*, Routledge & Keg Paul, London & Boston, pp. 109–28.

Beard, Mary Ritter, 1977, *A Source Book*, Ann J. Lane (ed.), Schocken Books, New York.

de Beauvoir, Simone, 1949: 1972, *The Second Sex*, Penguin, Harmondsworth, Middlesex.

Bernikow, Louise, 1980, *Among Women*, Harmony Books, New York.

Billington-Greig, Teresa (n. d.), *Suffragist Tactics: Past and Present*, Women's Freedom League, London.

Bryant, Margaret, 1979, *The Unexpected Revolution*, University of London.

Byrne, Eileen, 1978, *Women and Education*, Tavistock, London.

Cimons, Marlene, 1980a, 'Memories of a Pioneering Suffragette', *Los Angeles Times*, 16 January.

Cimons, Marlene, 1980b, 'Looking Back With America's Last Suffragette', *San Francisco Chronicle*, 6 February.

Cook, Blanche Wiesen (ed.), 1978, *Crystal Eastman on Women and Revolution*, Oxford University Press.

Davies, Margaret Llewelyn (ed.) 1915, *Maternity: Letters from Working Women*, G. Bell & Sons, London; reprinted 1978, Virago, London.

Davies, Margaret Llewelyn (ed.) 1931, *Life as We Have Known It: By Co-operative Working Women*, The Hogarth Press, London; reprinted 1977, Virago, London.

Dyhouse, Carol, 1981, *Girls Growing Up in Late Victorian and Edwardian England*, Routledge & Kegan Paul, London.

Eastman, Crystal, 1927: 1978, 'What shall we do with the "Woman's Page"?' *Time and Tide*, 20 May reprinted 1978, *On Women and Revolution*, Blanche Wiesen Cook (ed.), Oxford University Press.

Ehrenreich, Barbara and Deirdre English, 1978, *For Her Own Good: 150 Years of the Experts' Advice to Women*, Anchor Press, Doubleday, New York; 1979, Pluto Press, London.

Komarovsky, Mirra, 1953, *Women in the Modern World: Their Education and Their Dilemmas*, Little Brown, Boston.

Langdell, Cheri Davis (ed.) 1983, *Writing Against the Current*, Pandora Press, London.

Mackinnon, Catharine, 1979, *Sexual Harassment of Working Women*, Yale University Press, New Haven and London.

Marcus, Jane, 1980a, 'The Divine Right to be Didactic', in Elizabeth Robins, *The Convert*, The Women's Press, London, pp. v–xvi.

Marcus, Jane, 1980b, 'Introduction' to Rebecca West, *The Judge*, Virago, London, pp. 3–8.

Marcus, Jane, (ed.) 1982, *The Young Rebecca: Writings of Rebecca West 1911–1917*, Macmillan, London.

Matthews, Jacquie, 1983, 'Barbara Bodichon: Integrity in Diversity', in Dale Spender (ed.) *Feminist Theorists*, The Women's Press, London.

Matthews, Jacquie, (forthcoming), *Barbara Bodichon*, Pandora Press, London.

McWilliams-Tullberg, Rita, 1975, *Women at Cambridge: A Men's University – Though of a Mixed Type*, Victor Gollancz, London.

Morrell, Caroline, 1981, *'Black Friday' and Violence Against Women in the Suffragette Movement*, Women's Research and Resources Centre Publication, London.

Myrdal, Alva and **Klein, Viola,** 1956, *Women's Two Roles*, Routledge & Kegan Paul, London.

Porter, Cathy, 1980, *Alexandra Kollontai: A Biography*, Virago, London.

Ravetz, Alison, 1983 (in press), 'The Trivialisation of Mary Wollstonecraft: a personal and professional career re-vindicated', *Women's Studies International Forum*.

Ray, Gordon, N., 1974, *H. G. Wells and Rebecca West*, Macmillan, London.

Reimer, Eleanor, (forthcoming): Eleanor Reimer is currently working on a biography of Josephine Butler, and an account of the feminist network that was behind the repeal of the Contagious Diseases Acts.

Rich, Adrienne, 1980, *On Lies, Secrets and Silence*, Virago, London.

Robins, Elizabeth, 1907, *The Convert*, Methuen, London; reprinted 1980, The Women's Press, London.

Robins, Elizabeth, 1923, 'Six Point Group Supplement, The Six Points and Their Common Centre' *Time and Tide*, January, p. 60.

Rover, Constance, 1967a, *The Punch Book of Women's Rights*, Hutchinson, London.

Rover, Constance, 1967b, *Women's Suffrage and Party Politics in Britain 1866–1914*, Routledge & Kegan Paul, London.

Rover, Constance, 1970, *Love, Morals and the Feminists*, Routledge & Kegan Paul, London.

Rover, Constance, 1982, Interview with Dale Spender, Hythe, Kent, March.

Rowe, Marsha (ed.) 1982, *Spare Rib Reader*, Penguin, Harmondsworth, Middlesex.

Rowland, Robyn, 1983, *Women Who Do and Women Who Don't . . . Join the Women's Movement*, Pandora Press, London.

Russell, Dora, 1925, *Hypatia or Woman and Knowledge*, Kegan, Paul, Trench & Trubner, London.

Russell, Dora, 1927, 1928, *The Right to Be Happy*, Harper, New York and London.

Russell, Dora, 1965, 'In a man's world: The Eclipse of Woman', *Anarchy*, 56, vol. 5, no. 10, October, pp. 289–310.

Russell, Dora, 1974, 'The Long Campaign', *The New Humanist*, p. 257.

Russell, Dora, 1977, *The Tamarisk Tree: My Quest for Liberty and Love*, vol. I, Virago, London.

Russell, Dora, 1981, *The Tamarisk Tree: My School and the Years of War*, vol. II, Virago, London.

Russell, Dora, 1980, 'A Great Revolutionary Leader', *New Society*, 28 February, pp. 460–1.

Russell, Dora, 1982, Interview with Dale Spender, Cornwall, March.

Russell, Dora, forthcoming, *The Religion of the Machine Age*, Routledge & Kegan Paul, London.

Russell, Dora, forthcoming, *A Dora Russell Reader*, Pandora Press, London.

Sarah, Elizabeth, 1983, 'Christabel Pankhurst: Reclaiming Her Power', in Dale Spender (ed.), *Feminist Theorists*, The Women's Press, London.

Scott, Rivers, 1972, 'Rebecca West: Women's Lib and Why I'm For It', *The Sunday Telegraph*, 24 December, p. 6.

Showalter, Elaine, 1977, *A Literature of Their Own: British Women Novelists from Brontë to Lessing*, Princeton University Press, New Haven; 1978, Virago, London.

Smith, Dorothy, 1978, 'A Peculiar Eclipsing: Women's Exclusion from Man's Culture', *Women's Studies International Quarterly*, vol. I, no. 4, pp. 281–96.

Smyth, Jeanette, 1972, 'Half a Century of Feminism', *Washington Post*, 2 July.

Spedding, Carole and **Amanda Sebastyen,** 1982, 'Decades: Talking Across the Century', in Marsha Rowe (ed.) *Spare Rib Reader*, Penguin, Harmondsworth, Middlesex, pp. 603–6.

Spender, Dale, 1980, *Man Made Language*, Routledge & Kegan Paul, London and Boston.

Spender, Dale (ed.), 1981, *Men's Studies Modified: The Impact of Feminism on the Academic Disciplines*, Pergamon Press, Oxford.

Spender, Dale, 1982a, *Invisible Women: The Schooling Scandal*, Writers & Readers, London.

Spender, Dale, 1982b, *Women of Ideas and What Men Have Done to Them: from Aphra Behn to Adrienne Rich*, Routledge & Kegan Paul, London and Boston.

Spender, Dale, (ed.), 1983, *Feminist Theorists: Three Centuries of Women's Intellectual Traditions*, The Women's Press, London.

Spender, Lynne, 1983, *Intruders on the Rights of Men: Women's Unpublished Heritage*, Pandora Press, London.

Spry, Amanda (forthcoming), *Who's the Proper Feminist?*

Stanton, Elizabeth Cady, 1898a, *Eighty Years and More: Reminiscences 1815–1897*, T. Fisher Unwin, London: reprinted 1975, Schocken Books, New York.

Stanton, Elizabeth Cady (and the Revising Committee), 1898b, *The Woman's Bible*, European Publishing, New York; reprinted 1978 (6th printing) Coalition Task Force on Women and Religion, Seattle.

Stanton, Elizabeth Cady, Anthony, Susan B. and **Gage, Matilda Joslyn** (eds), 1881, *History of Woman Suffrage*, vol. I, Fowler & Wells, New York; reprinted 1969, Arno, The New York Times, New York.

Stopes, Marie, 1918, *Wise Parenthood*, A. C. Fairfield, London.

Stott, Mary, 1975, *Forgettings No Excuse*, Virago, London.

Stott, Mary (with Josephine King), (eds), 1977, *Is This Your Life? Images of Women in the Media*, Virago, London.

Stott, Mary, 1978, *Organization Woman: The Story of the National Union of Townswomen's Guilds*, Heinemann, London.

Stott, Mary, 1982, Interview with Dale Spender, London, March.

Strachey, Barbara, 1980, *Remarkable Relations: The Story of the Pearsall-Smith Family*, Victor Gollancz, London.

Symons, Julian, 1982, 'A Place in the Sun', *The Sunday Times*, 22 May.

Walters, Anna, 1977, 'The Value of the Work of Elizabeth Gaskell for Study at Advanced Level', unpublished MA dissertation, University of London, Institute of Education.

West, Rebecca, 1933, 'Mrs Pankhurst: A Reed of Steel', *The Post Victorians* (introduction by W. R. Inge) Ivor, Nicholson & Watson, London, pp. 479–500.

West, Rebecca, 1982a, *The Young Rebecca: Writings of Rebecca West 1911–1917*, Jane Marcus, (ed.), Macmillan, London.

West, Rebecca, 1982b, Interview with Dale Spender, London, March.

West, Rebecca, 1982c, *1900*, Weidenfeld & Nicolson, London.

Woolf, Virginia, 1928, *A Room of One's Own*, Hogarth Press, London; reprinted 1974, Penguin, Harmondsworth, Middlesex.
Woolf, Virginia, 1929, 'Women and Fiction', *The Forum*, March; reprinted 1972, Leonard Woolf, (ed.) *Virginia Woolf: Collected Essays*, Chatto & Windus, London, pp. 141–8.
Woolf, Virginia, 1938, *Three Guineas,* The Hogarth Press, London.

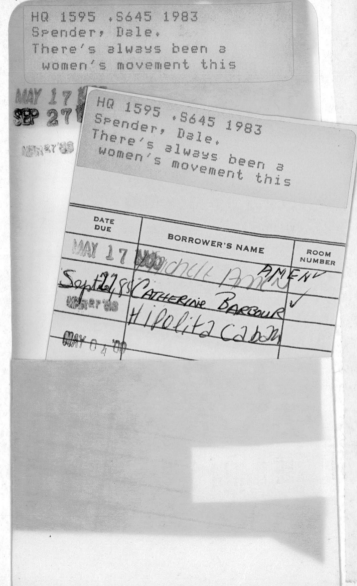